How to Get Rich; Without Winning the Lottery

A Guide to Money & Wealth Building

Barbara A. Friedberg, MBA, MS

Free Bonus:
How to Invest and Outperform
Most Active Mutual Fund Managers ($9.99 value).
(http://forms.aweber.com/form/87/2066025387.htm)

What people are saying about
"How to Get Rich;
Without Winning the Lottery"

"Friedberg's How to Get Rich, describes the basics of accumulating wealth in 7 broad steps. Her real life stories and multiple worksheets and quizzes bring home the message. Any young person without a good financial upbringing will benefit from her introductory book. It is a good reminder for the rest of us as well."

~ **Marie Phillips,** author of
"Choose Wealth! Be a Millionaire by Midlife"

"Excellent and comprehensive introductory money book. Great for someone just starting out to learn money basics. The book touches on the basic money topics in an engaging manner. The examples make the text come to life. The debt worksheet gets the reader moving fast, to get rid of debt. The housing worksheet helps differentiate between wants and needs in the housing area. The investment section in particular, cuts out the fluff and gets right to the point of how one gets rich."

~ J. Wang

"I really enjoyed reading this book. Even though Barbara uses simple language, the book is comprehensive and profound. Friedberg is a highly experienced personal finance professional."

~ **Nikita Brodskiy,** co-founder SavedPlus app

"It provides clear explanations of personal finance fundamentals, discusses good habits behind building wealth and illustrates many concepts with real life stories from the author's life. The story about moving from Southern California to the Mid-West was a vivid confirmation that Friedberg follows the principles she describes in the book."

~ **Leo Ostapiv,** author of "Home Finances for Couples"

Barbara Friedberg, MS, MBA is a former portfolio manager and university finance instructor. She is the editor of *Personal Finance; An Encyclopedia of Modern Money Management,* writes for *U.S. News & World Report,* and is the publisher of the Barbara Friedberg Personal Finance.com money and investing website.

How to Get Rich;
Without Winning the Lottery

Finally, a stand-alone guide designed for the individual who doesn't know the difference between debt and credit or a stock and a bond. This how-to-get-rich primer gets you started on the road to affluence in an easy-to-understand, step-by-step process for amassing wealth. Filled with examples and worksheets, you'll learn how to turn income into wealth whether you're self-employed or a company employee.

Getting rich doesn't happen overnight, and there is no secret to amassing wealth. But with *"How to Get Rich; Without Winning the Lottery"* you'll have the investing-decision essentials to help you navigate your own path to financial security.

Your chances of winning the jackpot on one ticket, according to the Powerball lottery website, are 1 in 175,223,510. If you're content with winning $100 bucks, your chances improve to 1 in 12,245. Please stop playing the lottery now in the hope of hitting the big one. The odds don't lie, and you are wasting money which could grow into real wealth for your future.

No matter what your lifestyle, money management knowledge or financial education, you'll discover what it takes to accumulate more money than you could imagine.

It's never too late to develop smart money strategies. Get started today, and let this book be your guide to developing wealth-building habits for tomorrow.

Contents

Introduction:
Get Started Now

"Money, if it does not bring you happiness,
will at least help you be miserable in comfort."

Helen Gurley Brown

The essence of getting rich is creating smart money habits to build a better life, free of financial worry. Begin to amass wealth with straightforward steps. Learn how to accumulate more money than you could imagine by developing wealth building habits.

No one is immune from making poor financial decisions. A few former $100,000 income earners who lost their jobs are regulars at our local soup kitchen. Lottery winners and professional athletes go bankrupt. On the other extreme, an unmarried school teacher recently left millions to a university in her will.

What's the difference between the wealthy and the rest?

The difference is creating and maintaining a wealth building mindset. How to get rich can be learned, just like how to ski, or how to speak another language. The wealthy delay gratification and understand how to transfer earnings from today into money for the future.

This isn't a "get rich quick" scheme; it is a guide to creating a wealthy life and leveraging what you already have with behaviors that build your net worth. There are several facets to building wealth. First you need income from a salary or self-employment.

Second, develop a plan to eliminate debt, without which getting rich is almost impossible. Next create the systems to turn your earnings into future wealth. Finally, live a meaningful life by making financial choices aligned with your priorities. Your income doesn't need to be tremendous, to get rich. Many individuals get rich on average incomes. The way you spend and live determine whether you end up rich or poor. *How to Get Rich* teaches you the tricks and secrets to get rich and still live a satisfying life.

Getting rich means something different to each of us. CNN reporter Jack Cafferty recently asked his viewers, "How much money would it take for you to feel wealthy"?[1] One reader needed enough for his family to "live comfy, not millions". Another reader set her feeling wealthy number at about 3 million.

Over the years, I made tons of money mistakes. I spent money on the wrong things, ordered courses and clothing online and paid way too much. Luckily, the mistakes didn't sink me. In fact, that $300 course I bought at age 24 on wealth building paid off in unexpected ways. First, I learned that $300 is an exorbitant sum to drop on information which I could have picked up in several $20 self-help personal finance books (or a $99 course). A $300 one time spending mistake is nothing compared with regularly buying expensive items on credit or splurging on a luxury car you can't afford. My smart money decisions and habits trumped the mistakes and over time, I amassed enough money for retirement, travel, and an enjoyable life, all on a reasonable income.

Learn the basics here and you are set for life. Each step tackles an important money topic. Put them all together and you have an action plan for lifelong wealth. Worksheets and clear directions create a no fail path to end up rich, while sacrificing the things that don't really matter.

This get rich instruction manual will teach you to face your bad money habits, and replace them with better ones. You'll learn how to attack growing debt and credit card bills. Explore solutions to live beneath your income and still have fun. The engaging worksheets teach how to manage your money and get on with life. This is your get rich instruction manual.

DOES MONEY EQUAL HAPPINESS?

Research abounds proving that more money does not equal happiness. In fact, the widely cited 2010 study of money and happiness by Princeton University's Deaton and Kahneman[2] found that above an income of $75,000, more money does not equal more happiness. Probably because below that benchmark, families feel financial issues impinge upon their ability to enjoy life. Strikingly, those making more than $75,000 are no happier than those making $75,000.

On the flip side, too much debt and poor spending habits are like wearing lead shoes in the pool. No matter how hard you kick, you still end up underwater. Regardless of your income, if you spend more than you earn, you will drown in debt and stress.

Make your life rock by creating smart money habits now. Learn the secrets to money. Find out how some folks never seem to have enough and others live amazing lives on small paychecks! You'll be surprised to uncover who amasses the greatest wealth over time, and it's not always those with the highest salaries.

How to Get Rich addresses the fast paced style of today by breaking down complex information into vital nuggets. In my money micro book, *How to Invest and Outperform Most Active Mutual Fund Managers*[3] I demonstrated that investing is neither difficult nor time consuming (contrary to the hordes of investment advisors telling you otherwise). This book follows that same solution oriented approach.

CRUCIAL SECRET TO WEALTH BUILDING

As a girl, at homework time, I procrastinated and avoided. My homework was too overwhelming, so I put it off. Locked in my room, I read, snacked, and talked on the phone. By nighttime, I was tired so I went to bed only to arise at 5:00 am and slap together some semblance of homework. Needless to say, this approach failed. I was stressed and miserable. There had to be a better way. Clearly, avoiding unpleasant tasks does not work out.

In the same way, running from debt or looking at your credit card statements, makes you feel awful. There is a better way.

Over time, I learned to break down my homework into small tasks and focus on one segment at a time. This strategy calmed my anxiety and to this day, this singular habit allows me to be quite productive. I subsequently went on to finish college and obtain two masters degrees.

Poor money habits are similar to my excessive procrastination.

The more you practice them, the worse your money management becomes and the worse you feel. The shift from procrastinator to achiever didn't happen overnight, but over time. The takeaway from my rough start is to take one small step at a time towards smart money behavior. In the end, you'll form the habits for sound money management and eradicate financial stress.

How to Get Rich breaks down the wealth building strategies and instructs how to:

- Get rid of debt systematically and quickly.
- Have cash for emergencies, vacations, down payment for a home, and retirement.
- Spend smart on stuff you really want and squeeze the most out of every dollar.
- Buy the smallest amount of insurance at the cheapest price, to keep you covered.
- Make more money from the cash you invest.
- Live how the rich live. (And it's not extravagantly.)

Read about other folks like you who are living great and how they do it. Don't worry, even if you lack good money models or dislike numbers, *How to Get Rich* will be your guide to smart money management.

You do not need to know the ins and outs of credit card interest rates. Who cares if the Dow went up or down? Just be aware that when you don't pay your credit card balance off every month in full, you are throwing away lots of money. Not just a few dollars but thousands. That's one difference between being rich or poor!

Read the book fast, in a few short sittings. You'll be finished in no time. Skip over the sections that do not apply to you. There is no way out, to achieve financial success, you must learn personal finance. *How to Get Rich* teaches you how to set up the systems to build lifelong wealth. There is no jargon or complicated investing scenarios; take in only these essential financial rudiments.

Start today, implement the simple and quick money strategies and get on with your life!

Get money smart now, so that you do not spend your life worrying about whether you have enough money to pay the bills, have fun, or save. Live a life free of money stress.

Step 1:
Keep The Debt Devil
From Sweating You

"The only reason a great many American families don't own an elephant is that they have never been offered an elephant for a dollar down and easy weekly payments."

Mad Magazine

Get rid of the debt devil and follow me on the path toward financial salvation. Debt, like the devil's pitchfork is a pain in the ass. How far is the debt free Promised Land you ask? It's as close as that credit card you are itching to use.

We all know what happens when you have an itch, you scratch it. Well that helps, for a moment, and later it is worse. Acquiring debt is the same as scratching that itch, it feels great for a moment, and as the bills mount, so does the pain.

WHAT IS DEBT?

Debt is the money you owe when you buy something on credit. Charge anything with a credit card or borrow money from a bank or other lender, and you have debt. The problem with debt is the interest you pay to the lender for the privilege of borrowing the money.

When you want something, but do not have the cash on

hand to pay for it you might borrow the money. You could borrow for a car, an education, a flat screen television, a home, a vacation... the list is endless.

Debt equals a loan.

If you took out a loan to pay for college, you have debt.

Charge stuff with a credit card and don't pay the bill in full at the end of the month? You have debt.

Here's the problem with debt.

Did you ever walk into a car dealership to test drive a car? As you browse the $20,000 sticker price in complete shock, the friendly car sales person works to calm you down. After touting the exciting features of the car, she espouses the low monthly payments. Can you afford $322 per month she asks?

You think, $322 per month isn't bad, I can handle it!

Hold on a minute. What happened to your interest in the sticker price? After signing on the dotted line, you are stuck paying $322 per month for six years. For those without a calculator handy, that's a total of $23,184. You just shelled out an additional $3,184 in interest payments[1] and acquired a car payment every month for six years. That is a long time and a lot of money.

Whenever you finance a purchase, realize that not only does the monthly payment matter but so do the sales price and the interest payments.

On top of the car payment, you are responsible for tax and registration fees on the new car purchase, car insurance, maintenance, and gas.

Transportation is a must; after all you need to get to work. But, you do not need a brand new car. The wealthy spend wisely on big purchases. Consider this, if you save up for a big down payment, and buy a more economical model or even a pre-owned vehicle you will have a lot more money to save or spend on other things.

A SMALL CHANGE EQUALS A BIG GAIN

You will have a lot more money to save or spend on other things if you revise your "need for a new car".

See how much you can save if you purchase a three year old model for $10,000, save up for a $2,500 down payment. This small tweak cuts your loan amount from $20,000.00 to $7,500 and reduces the term of the loan from six to three years. The monthly payment drops from $322 to $225, and the total interest charges are reduced from $3,184 to $592. Best of all, after three years your car payments are gone. See how a small change leads to a large financial gain.

In New York Times best seller, *Your Money or Your Life*, authors Robin and Dominguez reported that debtors anonymous alleges that you take on debt to avoid feelings of deprivation, deny pain, sorrow, loss, anger, loneliness, and despair. There are pricey financial and emotional consequences from "retail therapy". The quick high of the shiny new purchase dissolves as the credit card bills pour in.

Yet not everyone takes on debt to fill an emotional void.

Some folks take on debt and shop too much for fun, convenience, or even out of boredom. Zac Bissonette, the author of *How to be Richer, Smarter, and Better Looking than your Parents* has no television and relates debt spending with watching too many television programs and advertisements. Television advertisements and fictional characters turn your attention to people who seem to have more than you do. Almost magically, you feel worse in comparison with these fabricated over consumers. Shopping and debt are not the solution to psychological manipulation by advertisers.

Regardless of the motivation, only you know if you're trying to fill a hole inside with more stuff. Taking on debt to create happiness never works. The quick emotional high of getting something new is quickly replaced with the heavy burden of too much debt. In fact, buying to make you happy has a long term paradoxical effect.

Debt leads to misery, not joy.

EARN MORE BY ELIMINATING DEBT

Look at debt as reducing your salary. If you buy something on credit and don't pay it off in the same month, you'll spend anywhere from 15 to 50 percent more for that purchase. With credit card in hand, would you continue to "charge" if your purchases decrease your salary and eliminated any future raises? Buy on credit and immediately boost the purchase price.

Grab the tools to learn how to have more money by getting rid of debt. "Step 1: Keep the Debt Devil from Sweating You" begins your get rich path. Getting rid of debt releases a huge barrier to wealth.

> Less debt equals greater wealth.

IS THERE GOOD DEBT?

Mortgage debt is fine most of the time. A mortgage loan used to buy a home is a good use of debt. Not only is there a possibility that the home will increase in value (appreciate) but the interest on the loan can be deducted from your income and lower your federal tax bill. In reality, when buying real estate, mortgage debt is a necessity as few have the funds to pay cash for a home.

Even though mortgage debt is generally considered responsible borrowing, don't borrow too much; make sure your monthly mortgage payment is smaller than 25 percent of your monthly gross income.

> Gross income is total personal income,
> before all of those pesky charges like, taxes,
> Social Security, & Medicare deductions.

And save at least 10 percent of the total purchase price of the home for your down payment. In reality, you are much better off making a 20 percent down payment and borrowing 80 percent for the mortgage loan.

Don't believe anyone who recommends taking on more debt than you are comfortable with. After all, you have to pay the money back, not anyone else! We bought several homes and condominiums throughout our lives and never bought a home for the full amount a bank said we could afford! How do they know what we can afford? If we spent 28 percent of our gross income on a mortgage payment, we could not afford to contribute to our retirement fund and take a vacation once in awhile.

You decide your spending priorities, not the bank.

Don't take out a mortgage loan unless you are certain you'll stay in the house or condo at least five years. We made this mistake once and it didn't turn out well.

We bought a beautiful brand new home in a tony suburb of Indianapolis. After moving from the expensive San Diego region, our real estate dollars went much further in the more affordable mid-west. Our new home was luxurious in comparison with our smaller attached home in California. We expected to stay in Indianapolis for a while, but later decided it was not for us. After securing employment elsewhere, we had to sell our two year old home.

We learned an expensive lesson when it came time to sell. Real estate was not appreciating very rapidly in price in Indianapolis.

Our home was decorated quite modern in a region partial to country style. Long story short- we took a large loss in the sale of our home. In the process, we learned three valuable lessons:

1. Only buy a home if you are certain you will be residing in the area for a minimum of five years, preferably longer.

2. When selling, stage your home to blend in with the style of the community.

3. Don't be greedy. We chose not to entertain our first offer because it was too low, and we ended up ultimately selling for less than the initial offer.

This was an example where borrowing money for a mortgage loan was a bad idea. We would have been better off renting until we were certain we'd remain in the area at least five years.

Student loan debt (in moderation) to equip you for a fruitful career is usually worth it. The college graduate earns almost 100 percent more money over a lifetime than the high school graduate, so taking on some debt to boost your earning power is okay. Remember, you have to pay the money back and you may not earn a bundle upon graduation, so keep borrowing to a minimum. Don't use your student loan to live in high style while going to college. You will regret it. Get a part time job and live economically to cut down on your borrowing costs.

Car loans can be minimized if you save up for large down payment and take out a short term loan. Realize, that a car depreciates (declines) in value every year. So don't get stuck paying a lot for a car whose value continues to fall. Believe it or not, you can save up for a few years and pay cash for a car.

Credit card debt is not all bad. When you pay the entire credit card bill in full (within the grace period) every month, you pay no interest or fees, and that's good. In my opinion, the only time to use a credit card is when you can pay off the entire balance in full every month. This is because credit card interest charges are high and by carrying a balance on your card, you increase the cost of every item you buy. Conversely, if you use your credit card and pay the bill off completely within the grace period, you will develop a solid credit history.

BAD DEBT

Do not borrow money for:

- Food

- Clothes

- Vacations

- Gifts

- Weddings

Save up, and if you don't have the cash, don't buy. It feels awful paying for something that you don't have any more. Do you even remember what you ate at the fancy restaurant last month? If not, why should you continue to pay for it now?

Never borrow to impress. Figure out how to feel better about yourself without overspending.

> Rule of thumb, if you are borrowing for something that will be worth less in the future, wait to buy until you can pay cash.

Charge a fancy vacation, extravagant restaurant meals, expensive clothes, and if you don't pay for them in the month you buy them, expect to pay up to 50 percent or more in interest payments on top of the original purchase price. Interest charges and fees add up quickly. It's not worth paying $200 for a $100 pair of shoes. Why not get a similar pair on sale for $50 cash and save yourself $150? I promise you will be much happier in the long run without the debt!

WHAT'S WRONG WITH DEBT?

You may be thinking, "It seems like everyone has debt, it can't be that bad." Actually, a friend of mine said that to me. She got quite an earful in response. She's still my friend, so I guess it wasn't too much advice.

Take a look at Josh. He loves electronics, computer games, and entertainment. Josh believes that since he has a job, he should reward himself by buying whatever he wants. The credit card companies must agree, since they continue to send him applications for new cards. Like most ambitious adults, Josh would like to go on nice vacations, get married, and buy a home in the future.

Josh isn't a big planner and he's happy he graduated from college and got a job.

Without even trying, he racked up $1,000 credit card debt on the latest tablet computer and flat screen television. When the credit card bill arrives, he pays a bit more than the minimum each month while adding a few extra charges to his card along the way. Josh has lots of great stuff and an awesome time going to clubs and eating out with friends.

Now $1,000 doesn't sound like too much debt. You probably know lots of friends with $1,000 debt.

Every month that you do not pay that debt off in full, you are charged interest by the credit card company for the privilege of using the money they lent you. At Josh's 20 percent interest rate, the credit card company tacks on 20 percent to any balance left on the card.

Let's look at how it plays out by paying a few bucks over the minimum payment[2]. Also, assume Josh decides not to add any additional charges and stops using his credit card completely.

- Current debt = $1,000
- Interest rate paid to credit card company = 20%
- Monthly payment = $30
- Months to pay = 49 (that's over 4 years)
- Total interest paid = $470
  (on top of the original $1,000)

By the time the $1,000 purchases were completely paid off, the stuff he bought was obsolete and instead of paying the original price of $1,000, he paid the exorbitant sum of $1,470! It's hard to believe that paying only $30 per month increases the total cost by about 50 percent and takes over four years to pay off the credit card bill.

Josh doesn't like that scenario and decides to tighten his belt and pay $150 per month towards his $1,000 debt and stops using the card!

- Current debt = $1,000
- Interest rate paid to credit card company= 20%
- Monthly payment = $150
- Months to pay = 7
- Total interest paid = $50

In the second example, Josh cut back in other areas and found $150 each month to put towards his debt. He didn't charge anything else. In seven months he got rid of the credit card debt.

See here's the deal; if you only pay the minimum payment, and don't add to the balance, you end up paying a lot of interest. Josh paid a couple of bucks more than the minimum in the first example and paid an additional $470 in interest on top of the original $1,000.

Would you buy those same electronics if they cost 50 percent more than you originally paid? I don't think so.

Increase your credit card payment,
and get rid of debt fast.

THE PERILS OF CREDIT CARD DEBT

Paying interest on top of the purchase price as Josh did, is literally throwing money away. If you have the cash to buy a $1,000 game console and television now, great, go on and get it. If you don't have the money now, save up, and buy it when you have the cash in hand!

When you buy on credit you multiply the purchase price.

Try this experiment; ask your grandparents how they paid for their first car. I bet they paid cash! In fact, my husband's parents never borrowed money for anything.

By wasting money on unnecessary interest payments, just so you can buy something NOW, you are making a choice to GIVE UP THE ABILITY TO BUY SOMETHING ELSE. This concept is called the "opportunity cost." By spending money on something, you're giving up the opportunity to buy something else.

What else could Josh have done with the $470 interest payments?

If he invested that $470 for five years in a stock mutual fund and received a 7% return, his $470 would be worth $660. That's enough for a nice, memorable vacation, or a new computer!

If he used the money for interest payments, at the end of five years, he would have a five year old television and an obsolete tablet computer.

Which would you choose? Save up and buy an affordable television or tablet with cash and invest the $470 you did not spend on interest payments. Or buy expensive electronics on credit and devote four years and $470 to interest payments.

If you're still not convinced that debt slams your future wealth and peace of mind, I'd be happy to loan you my own money at 20 percent per year.

HOW TO GET RID OF DEBT

Do you get it? Less debt equals more money! Interest payments are like flushing money down the toilet! Even debt for a good purpose like education should be paid off as quickly as possible.

Like dieting, there are many varieties of loan repayment. What works for your roommate may not work for you. That said, unless you are earning an abundance of cash, practice the following maxim.

In order to pay off your debts quickly, you must delay gratification. In fact, all success depends on patience and persistence. How you pay off your loans is less important than making it a priority to get rid of all debt (except mortgage debt) as fast as possible.

MOTIVATION

Right now, reading this inspiring book, you're all set to cut up the cards and go on an all cash program. Great, but how do you keep the motivation going? The next trip to the mall or visit to Amazon.com will likely set the dreams of more and better stuff into gear.

Making life changes is about habit change.

Your motivation waxes and wanes.

Develop good habits, practice them and they become permanent. Motivation then becomes immaterial. I can give you an outline of one way to kick the debt to the curb, but only you decide if you are willing to delay gratification and get control of your money.

Follow this easy debt reduction plan or find one of your own. The best way to tackle any change is bit by bit, so attack one step at a time. It's overwhelming to look at all the steps at once.

Get started, no matter how you feel.

GET OF RID OF DEBT

Figure out how much debt you have. If you don't know how much you owe, then how will you know how fast you can pay it off? Include student loan debt, credit card debt, and all other loans. This step may be scary and difficult. Accept the challenge and realize that the feelings of control are worth the temporary discomfort of confronting the debt.

Pull out every debt and credit card statement for all debt and complete this chart NOW. Use Bankrate.com for debt payoff calculators.[2]

Barbara Friedberg Personal Finance-DEBT CHART ©

Name of Account	Total Balance Due	Payment due Date	Minimum Payment	Interest Rate	NOTES
Bank of America Visa	$2,000	15th of the month	$80	13%	Pay minimum: 30 months to pay off debt Pay $240: 9 months to pay off

When you pay triple the minimum payment you cut the payoff from two and a half years to nine months.

Figure out how much you owe today, follow this plan, and

start paying down your debt. Be realistic. If your take home pay is $2,500 per month, don't expect to make $1,200 debt repayments per month, unless you decide to move in with mom and dad.

BARBARA'S DEBT REDUCTION PLAN:

- Do not take on any additional debt. Put your credit cards away! Cut up all but one or two, stick them in water and put in the freezer.

- Pay at least triple on the smallest debt every month.

- Pay the minimum payment on all of the others.

- When one debt is paid off, treat yourself to a free or cheap reward. Consider a visit to the dollar store or a long hike at a nature park. Choose something that's a real treat for you. Don't skip this step. Too much deprivation is unsustainable and a small reward keeps your debt payment on track.

- Start all over and pay triple on your next smallest balance and continue until paid off.

- As you get in the habit of paying down your debt, and your confidence grows, try this approach to speed up the debt repayment. Tackle the highest interest rate debt.

When debt is strangling you, it's important to pay more than the minimum payment, or you will never be able to save. Put all pay raises, tax refunds, and unexpected income towards your debt.

Keep at it; do not quit paying down the debt. And stop using the credit cards.

> As long as you carry credit card debt,
> no matter how much you save, you lose! You gain more
> financially by eliminating credit card debt balances
> than by saving. Pay off debt first, and then save.

Step 2:
Saving-The Path
To More Benjamins

"Too many people spend money they haven't earned, to buy things they don't want, to impress people they don't like."

Will Smith

WHY SAVE?

Do you have all the money you need to buy what you want currently and in the future? If so, drop this book now and get on with your life.

If you need money for car repairs, new clothes, vacations, electronics, child rearing, new car, hobbies, entertainment, a home, or retirement, this section will get you started.

There was a picture in the newspaper (I know, who reads the newspaper anymore?) this morning about Alex, a successful sales executive smiling in front of a high end luxury car. It was difficult to muster up sympathy for Alex. Alex had an outstanding sales career and earned $100,000 per year.

And then Alex got fired.

You're probably thinking as I did, "So what?" He can retire or at least look for part time work if he can't get another full time job. After all, with that nice salary, he must have a large amount saved up.

Wrong!

Alex had $5,000 saved up. That's right; a guy making 100 grand only saved $5,000!

Throughout his life, he spent what he earned and did not save for the future. Now, he is terrified and can't find work. Think it'll be easy for Alex to get a new job? Think again; most companies would rather hire a younger person with a likelihood of working for the company for a while, than a sixty five year old with a big gut.

Alex is faced with living another twenty years with only a modest social security payment to get him by.

Is that the life you want for yourself?

I DON'T MAKE ENOUGH MONEY TO SAVE

Take this quiz if you believe you don't make enough money to save.

Barbara Friedberg Personal Finance
DO YOU MAKE ENOUGH MONEY TO SAVE QUIZ?©
Place a checkmark in either the Yes or No Column

	Yes	No
Have you bought a coffee and bag of chips at a convenience store this month?		
Do you eat meals out more than two or three times per month?		
Is your phone bill hovering around the one hundred dollar mark?		
Are you at the clubs and bars with your friends a few times per week?		
Is the mall your regular hang out?		
Do you see your hairdresser more than your closest friends?		
Do your sneakers sport the name of a big time basketball player?		
Do you believe that others must think you look wealthy?		

SCORING;

Count up the number of YES answers.

If you scored more than 1 YES answer, then you have enough money to save.

As a volunteer tax preparer for lower income folks, I was amazed at the frequency during which the clients came in with a convenience store snack; small pack of cheese crackers, a soda, a candy bar, or another quick item. In contrast, before my three hour shift, I packed a drink and snack for myself at home.

Now, I'm not saying this to gloat, but to inform that, the

money lost is substantial by buying snacks out instead of bringing from home. Slap together a few bad money habits; smoking, buying lunch out, playing the lottery and you've needlessly spent thousands of dollars over the years.

Look at the daily cost of convenience store snacks:

Coffee from a shop:	$2.00
Sweet roll:	$2.00
Pack of crackers and cheese:	$1.25
Soda:	$1.70
Total:	$6.95

Compare that with snacks brought from home:

Coffee:	$.50
Cereal or donut:	$.75
A few crackers with some peanut butter or cheese on them:	$.75
Soda (can from home):	$.25
Total:	$2.25

Daily Savings:	$4.70

Multiply $4.70 by 365 days and that's $1,715 wasted in a year. Invest the $1,715 each year in a stock mutual fund returning 7 percent.[3] At the end of 20 years, the $1,715 annual investment is worth $70,307.

Is it worth planning and spending a few minutes each day to pack some snacks and a lunch, in order to invest for the future?

Stock up on low cost snacks at the grocery and leave them in the car or at work. We leave a flat of waters and coke in the car so we don't have to pay $2.00 for a can of soda. If you think it takes too much work and planning, ask yourself if doing a bit of planning is worth $70,307.

> In *The Difference*, Jean Chatzky found that 55 percent
> of the self-made rich attributed habitual saving
> to their financial success.

My dad was dirt poor growing up. He started work at age 10 selling newspapers on the street corners. His dad worked at a factory until he was laid off for six years. His family barely scraped by. Beginning with the first dollar dad made, he put part of his earnings into savings. No matter how much he earned, part went to savings. And if he didn't have cash to pay for something, he made due without.

Saving starts with your mind. Change your attitude and realize that saving is possible at any income. Learn ways to save so that you won't even miss the cash.

It's easy to retrain your habits and build wealth.

THE SAVING HABIT; MONEY TIME AND CHOICES

Before tackling the nitty gritty of saving, consider your wealth in a global manner. In one way, you are as wealthy as the richest person on earth. Everyone has the same amount of time each day. No one gets more than 1,440 minutes per day. The wealthiest professional athlete has the same number of minutes each day that you do. Once a minute passes, no one can buy it back. So, actually, your time, not your money is the most valuable resource. You can make additional money, time is irreplaceable. Spent time is never refunded.

> Before spending time or money, think about how to maximize these precious resources.

Time and money spent both involve making choices. Pack a peanut butter sandwich and you give up the chance of grabbing a turkey sandwich at Subway. Go to the mall at 2:00 on Saturday and you forgo the chance to hike in the park. Not only does that decision reduce your physical activity for the time, but also ups the chance you'll buy something on impulse. Say yes to one thing and automatically say no to something else.

Just because time is irreplaceable, does not mean you can forget about saving cash and just worry about your time!

Both your time and your money have constraints. Time and money decisions are interwoven. Your current and future cash is limited. If you buy something now, you make a choice not to buy something else in the future. If you spend time on one activity now, you give up the opportunity to spend that time on another activity.

> Saving begins with your own priorities. Decide what is important to you first. Then allocate your money to the items of greatest importance.

Saving begins with a decision; a mental commitment to become financially secure. You will always be anxious and worried about money if you do not save. That anxiety and worry lowers your enjoyment of life. Consequently, money squandered on impulse buys increases stress levels.

Groundbreaking research by scholars Steven Venti of Dartmouth University and David Wise[1] of Harvard found that the greatest determinant of lifetime wealth is a person's savings rate. In their study of wealth accumulation at retirement they found low earning people who managed to save quite a large sum over their lifetimes and conversely, there were high earners with very little wealth accumulation. In other words, high earners who lived expensively and extravagantly during their lives ended up without much cash at retirement; kind of like that guy in the paper who made $100,000 per year and only saved $5,000.

Learn the savings habit. Developing any habit is difficult initially and gets easier over time. As one who is staring retirement in the face, I am happy I started saving regularly in my twenties. In fact, figuring out how to live large on a budget became a game for my husband and me. We figured out how to squeeze the most fun out of our meager earnings. Those happy hours with free hors d'oeuvres were our "go to" dinners out! Starting in our twenties we continued to live on less than we earned and planned our splurges.

I started out a bit of a mess. I was fat as a teen because I ate too much and didn't exercise enough. I was undisciplined, insecure, and plagued with self-doubts. I tried to diet by cutting back drastically; I was in a big hurry to lose the weight. The paradox about drastic change is that it rarely works. I managed to cut my calories to subsistence levels for a day or two, but then the hunger won out, and because of my deprivation, I splurged. During the summers, with no school and less stress, I dropped a lot of weight, only to regain the pounds in the fall and winter, spurred on by the pressures of school. The problem was that I didn't know how to handle the stressors in my life and so I used food as a coping strategy.

How similar were my weight loss troubles to spending and saving dilemmas?

Do you spend to deal with stress? Do you save dramatically for awhile, only to rebound from the deprivation into a spending binge? There is a better way.

Saving, like dieting requires a sensible lifestyle plan. Learn savings strategies and the money will pile up.

Write down your money goals, and increase your chance of getting rich.

PAINLESS SAVING STRATEGIES; HOW TO SAVE

> Jane Bryant Quinn came up with the smartest and easiest way to save. Have a predetermined amount automatically transferred from your paycheck into your bank, investment, retirement accounts. Period! That's it.

It is certain that if you don't have immediate access to the money, you will learn to live without it. This strategy begins with some effort, but once the initial set up is complete, the saving continues with ease.

This plan starts you on the path to lifetime wealth, and sets the groundwork for "Step 6: Be a Portfolio Player! I Have no Money Investing Strategy".

You may already have a bank account, credit union account, or workplace retirement account; if so, you're on the right path.

The difference between savings institutions, investment

brokers, and even credit card companies has blurred quite a bit. There are new venues for money management popping up daily. You can open a savings and checking account at a discount broker and you can purchase investments at a bank. It's all a bit confusing, so here's a handy chart to lay out the most popular options:

Barbara Friedberg Personal Finance
WHERE TO SAVE CHART ®

	Saving Products	How They Make Money	Details
BANK	Checking account, money market savings account, and certificates of deposit	For profit institution. Make money from fees, and the difference between interest received from borrowers and interest paid out to depositors.	Usually charge higher fees than credit unions. Have more branches than credit unions. Anyone can open an account. Online only banks may have lower fees and higher interest rates.
CREDIT UNION	Share checking account, money market savings account, and share term certificates of deposit	Not for profit, owned by depositors.	Have membership criteria. Fewer branches than banks. Usually have lower fees and higher interest rates than banks.
DISCOUNT BROKERAGE COMPANY	Checking account, money market savings account, and certificates of deposit	Varies by company.	Many discount brokers have same checking and saving options as banks and credit unions. No fee and interest checking also available.

Upon a quick visit to Charles Schwab, Fidelity, and PNC bank, the savings options were the same. So how do you choose where to put your money? The most important criteria for saving are ease of access and no fees (understand that the savings institution makes money by lending out your deposits, they shouldn't charge you for that privilege).

Choose a bank, credit union, or discount broker, either online or bricks and mortar or both based upon the fee structure, availability of ATM machines, and ease of making deposits. As interest rates rise, you'll want access to a money market fund for your savings, as they pay higher interest rates.

Do not obsess over your choice, the important part is getting started saving and keeping fees at bay, not worrying if you chose the "perfect" savings company.

QUICK START-PATH TO SAVING

Get started immediately by setting up your saving and investment accounts.

Step 1: Open up three accounts. Each account corresponds with a savings basket explained in the next sections. It's easiest to open up the three accounts at the same institution.

One account is for money needed for short term goals, usually less than four years. This might include money for a vacation, or a buildup of your emergency fund. I keep our short term goals money and emergency fund in the same account.

The second account is for medium term goals (five to ten years) such as college for the kids, home down payment or remodel, or new (used) car fund.

The third account is for long term money. These are funds you don't expect to touch for decades. Usually, this is your retirement money and might also include college savings for a younger child. This account might be your work place retirement account, 401(k), or 403(b).

Make it simple and open the three accounts at one or (at most) two institutions. Consider a discount broker such as Charles Schwab or TD Ameritrade which offers banking and investing services.

Where to open the three accounts for short, medium, and long term spending and saving:

- **Bank, credit union savings account, or discount investment brokerage account:** Short term goals
- **Bank, credit union savings account, or discount investment brokerage account:** Medium term goals
- **Investment/brokerage account-Roth IRA or 401(K)** (through work or on your own): Long term goals

Step 2: March into your personnel/human resources office and complete the paperwork to have a certain amount transferred from your paycheck into each of these three accounts. Bring financial institution account numbers and routing numbers. If your budget is tight, transfer a small amount to start, you can increase the monies transferred into each account later.

For the self-employed, open an individual Roth IRA at a discount broker. The Roth IRA is your retirement account. Obtain the paperwork from your bank and the broker. Have a set amount of money transferred monthly from checking into a savings account, for short and intermediate term needs, and a Roth IRA, for retirement.

Every month your savings allotment automatically goes into your accounts. After initial set up, you do nothing except update your Savings Chart. At the end of each month, write down how much you have saved toward each goal.

The next steps explain how to use this savings approach to maximize your wealth.

STEP BY STEP BASKET SAVING

Now that you have money flowing into each of your three saving/investing accounts, here's how you use the accounts to get rich.

The three basket approach aligns your money with the specific goals. It'll keep you from blowing the kids college savings on a vacation. The charts keep it simple.

BASKET 1: SHORT TERM SAVINGS

Where: Easy access funds go straight to the **bank, credit union, or discount brokerage.** Either bricks and mortar or online are fine.

What: Short term (one to four years) money goals. This basket holds money for short term necessary spending, emergencies, and planned splurge items. Be sure to include the emergency funds in your short term goals because there are always unexpected expenses.

Did I mention that the emergency fund is key?

Build this account up to six to nine months of living expenses. That way, if you lose your job or have a financial setback, you won't lose your home and will be able to pay your bills. Dip into this fund only for real emergencies! This money is not for more clubbing, fancy dinners out, and that cute $300 purse or tablet computer you must have. In fact, according to a *Money Magazine* article, "Get Happy in 2012", having an emergency fund was the greatest predictor of financial satisfaction.

Type: Don't worry about your interest rate on this ready access cash. Put the funds in a vanilla savings account or money market mutual fund. Use the chart to keep organized and on track. Update the chart monthly to motivate and keep you on track.

Another option for emergency funds is one of my favorite investments, Government I (inflation) Savings Bonds[2]. The bonds are guaranteed to protect your money from loss of value due to inflation and not taxed until the funds are withdrawn. Buy the bonds in denominations starting at $50 and purchase up to $10,000 worth per year. One caveat, you need to wait one year before redeeming the bonds, so start your purchase as soon as possible.

Barbara Friedberg Personal Finance-Basket 1©
Short term Savings Goals
Bank, Credit Union, Discount Investment Brokerage Account 1-4 Years

NAME	SAVING TARGET	AMOUNT SAVED
Emergency fund	$3,000	$1,000
Summer vacation	$1,000	$600

BASKET 2: MEDIUM TERM SAVINGS

Where: Easy access funds go straight to the **bank, credit union, or discount brokerage.** Either bricks and mortar or online are fine.

What: Medium (five to ten years) term money goals. Use this basket for college expenses for the teens or a home remodel. It's tempting to dip into this fund as the cash builds up. To keep from withdrawing your hard earned savings, don't look at the balance more than 3 or 4 times per year. No need to update this one monthly.

Type: Invest in a certificate of deposit (CD) or money market mutual fund to receive higher interest payments. Government I Savings Bonds, mentioned in the last section are also useful for this basket. I bonds preserve your purchasing power from inflation.

Barbara Friedberg Personal Finance-Basket 2©
Mid term Savings Goals

**Bank, credit Union, or
Discount Investment Brokerage Account
Certificate of Deposit, Money Market Mutual Fund,
I Bonds 5-10 Years**

NAME	SAVING TARGET	AMOUNT SAVED
Down payment on condo	*$20,000*	*$500*
Pay off student loans	*$10,000*	*$1,000*

BASKET 3: LONG TERM SAVINGS

Where: These funds are funneled into brokerage accounts through your workplace and/or personal investment accounts. The workplace retirement accounts are called 403(b), 401(k), or Roth IRA. Sometimes your employer matches your contributions into this fund. The employer match is free money. You must contribute up to the amount your employer contributes in order to receive the free cash.

If you don't have a workplace investment option, set up a Roth IRA on your own at a discount broker. As your income grows, consider contributing to both the workplace retirement account and an individual Roth IRA.

What: Long term retirement savings and goals in the distant future. This is for your long term funds; set it and forget it!

Type: Since you won't need this money for many years, invest your money in stock and bond index mutual funds to optimize your chances for growth. Expect an average of 7 percent growth per year with a balanced 65 percent stock fund and 35 percent bond fund allocation. You'll learn more about options for this basket in "Step 6: Be a Portfolio Player! I have no Money Investing Strategy". For even more investing information pick up my free micro book *How to Invest and Outperform Most Active Mutual Fund Managers*[3].

Barbara Friedberg Personal Finance-Basket 3© Long term Savings Goals		
Work Retirement and/or Discount Investment Brokerage Account Stock and Bond Index Mutual Funds 10 + Years		
NAME	SAVING TARGET	AMOUNT SAVED
Child's college expenses	*$60,000*	*$0*
Retirement	*$750,000*	*$4,000*

Once the accounts are set up, the funds transferred from paycheck to account, and the investment choices for Basket 3 are selected, the heavy lifting is complete. Monitor monthly expenses and funnel raises and tax refunds into the accounts.

This savings program sets you on a wealth building track.

HOW MUCH TO SAVE?

If you have a wad of cash in your hand, you will spend it. Yet, you aren't likely to spend money you don't see!

When I first started working, my co-worker and I would go to the bank with our paychecks every two weeks. I deposited part of the check into my savings account and the rest into the checking account for regular expenses.

My co-worker cashed hers. That's right, she cashed her entire paycheck! She walked out of the bank with a big wad of money.

That was the worst financial planning decision.

I am certain that she did not save. How likely do you think it is that she would return to the bank with money to put into a savings account later in the month? With that money in her pocket, I know it was spent before the next check arrived.

Your personal challenge is to find the optimal balance, for you, between spending now and saving for the future. The easiest method is to start saving 10 percent of your income.

> Money taken out of your paycheck before you see it will not be missed.

Learn to live on the rest!

Do not despair if you can't save 10 percent; save as much as you can now, even if it is just 2 percent of your income. In fact, it's better to save something now, no matter how small an amount rather than give up and save nothing. The simple act of transferring a part of your earnings into saving and investing accounts gets you in the habit of wealth building. As your income grows, so will your saving.

If you're not sure about how much to save for certain situations, there are lots of calculators to help. My favorite site for savings calculators is at bankrate.com.

One of my blog readers, Melissa from Mom'sPlans.com validated this approach with the comment,

"I love these tips. I had money automatically deducted and put into a savings account each paycheck. I noticed not having the money the first two paychecks, and then it was painless after that. Such a simple way to save."

Get in the habit of automatically saving each month; learn to live on what is left, and save more as your income grows. After the money is funneled into the saving and investing accounts, you're free to spend whatever is left. How easy is that?

Step 3:
Spend Your Way
To An Awesome Life

*"If you think the United States has stood still,
who built the largest shopping center in the world?"*

Richard M. Nixon

Shopping is intricately intertwined with modern culture. It's part of leisure, relaxation, and entertainment. Shopping out of necessity is rare. What if I told you that it's possible to tweak your spending a bit and build tens of thousands more dollars?

If you spend right it's possible to boost your wealth, but if you spend foolishly your money drifts away. You don't have to give up all luxuries to become rich. By spending strategically, you can have what matters most to you.

Have you made a big life change? Of course you have, every adult was once a child with few responsibilities or expectations. Somehow, you managed to grow up, get a job, and live on your own-all mammoth changes.

Spending smart is a new skill for many and can be learned. Approach careful spending as you would any other life choice. You need clothes, food, and someplace to live. How much you spend on those necessities directly correlates with how rich you will become.

My parents gave me an amazing gift; smart financial habits. Although I was trained since birth in wealth building, it is never too late to learn how to get rich. When I met my husband, he had never set foot in Wal-Mart, Target, Sears, or an outlet mall. He was brought up to believe that only poor people shopped at "those types of stores." One of our first fights was in Macy's when I suggested going to the outlet mall.

Flash forward several decades and my husband is the best shopper I know. He saw the new Mark Anthony line at Kohl's and was impressed with the style, and distressed with the prices. He said, "I am waiting until the end of season sales for this line of clothing to go on sale". Last week, at the summer close out, he picked up a black shirt and slacks at 90 percent off the original price. In fact, he is so astute that he has analyzed when and where to shop in order to get the greatest quality at the lowest price. In spite of his bargain shopping savvy, if you saw how well he dresses, you'd think he was a "luxury shopper."

BUY A MERCEDES FOR LESS THAN A FORD

My parents loved luxury cars: Cadillac's and Mercedes. Although they indulged in these extravagances, they paid cash for their gently used luxury cars. They rode around in style for a bargain price. Meticulous about maintenance, they kept their cars forever which kept their transportation costs rock bottom. Mom and dad spent less on transportation than many Ford owners while indulging in their penchant for high end cars.

Not only did dad hate to waste money but he abhorred wasting time. This led him to open an office near home. He kept his commute below 15 minutes, cutting down on time and gas. These lifestyle decisions saved money, saved time, and left more money for investing and building his business.

THE WRONG PATH

My husband and I lived next to an affluent neighborhood filled with mansions, private pools, big yards and the rest. Our home was comfortable and attractive yet definitely lower priced and sized than our neighbors. On his annual visit, the carpet cleaner told me a story regarding the mansions across the way.

Mr. Carpet Cleaner mentioned that the interiors of many of those homes are practically unfurnished! I was shocked at this information. How could those expensive lavish homes lack furniture? Weren't the owners' high income earners with money to burn? I assumed the purchasers of these large homes were highly compensated doctors from the neighboring medical center and high level corporate executives.

The carpet cleaner's disclosure confirmed a finance truism; smart money management is not only for the low income, it is for all.

Even high earners go bankrupt along with big time lottery winners. If you confuse living rich with actually accumulating wealth, then financial failure ensues. Looking wealthy is not the path to accumulating wealth. Dr. Thomas J. Stanley of *Millionaire Next Door* fame found millionaires were difficult to pick out from the crowd. The millionaires were not the ones living extravagantly, but look just like middle income folks. I guess that's how they became millionaires.

If you overspend, forgo saving, lack insurance, and live beyond your means, regardless of your income level, you will experience money problems.

How you spend directly influences how rich you will become. Smart spending gives you more for less. Spend wisely with thought and discipline and contentment follows. According to Malkiel and Ellis in *The Elements of Investing*, saving gives you the tools to get more of what you want, need, and enjoy. How you spend, impacts whether you feel satisfied or deprived. How to get rich is about maximizing your resources, not deprivation.

Hunger for luxury goods on a small income and you will always feel "less than." Switch your material wishes to align with your funds, and you will feel wealthy. Personally, I shop at sales, outlet stores, and lower priced trendy shops. By saving on clothes, there's more money left to save, invest, and get rich.

CASE STUDY: WHAT WOULD YOU DO?

While at the mall, I overheard a mom and her 15 year old daughter discussing winter boots. The daughter was at the full price boot table. She begged her mom for a $200 pair, but was also interested in the $125 pair. The mom made her daughter an offer, you can have the $125 pair today, but if you want the $200 pair, you'll have to wait until I get paid next week.

I was fascinated with the exchange. The mom clearly believed that getting her daughter (who will probably outgrow the boots next year) a $200 pair of boots was just fine. Additionally, she did not have the money now to pay for them. (Or, maybe her budgeted shoe allowance was already met for the month.)

My concerns:

- If her budget was so tight that she did not have the

funds available to pay for the boots, was she really wealthy enough to buy her daughter $200 boots?

- Did she have an adequate emergency fund?
- Was she saving for retirement?
- Was her daughter learning to define herself by what she owned and not who she was as a person?

I was buying my daughter boots, too. I have enough cash in the budget to buy her $200 boots. That said, spending $200 on boots is sending my kid the wrong message. We shopped around and found a pair on sale for $90. I don't think she enjoyed the $90 boots any less than $200 boots.

> How you spend does not determine who you are.
> If you buy more expensive things, you are not
> a more worthy person.

Your spending, saving, and investing habits, not your income determine whether you will amass wealth or not. There are individuals on modest salaries who have amassed great amounts of wealth through smart lifestyle, saving, and spending choices.

Dr. Charles Richards in *The Psychology of Wealth* asked this question, "How many of my behaviors have I not 'voted on'? What am I doing that I didn't consciously choose to do yet continue to do every day?" Question your actions and their subsequent outcomes, recommends Darren Hardy in *The Compound Effect*. If you're surrounded by a pool of expensive things, paid for with credit, consider the choices you made to arrive at the material and debt excess. You have ultimate control of your choices. It's no surprise that there is a direct correlation between how you spend and how rich you become.

My dad's best friend, John died recently with a $10,000,000 estate. Can you guess his occupation? What would you imagine? That he was a businessman, entrepreneur, or highly compensated executive? He was a salaried IRS employee for his entire career. John amassed his wealth through smart investing and economical living. John lived modestly and invested shrewdly. I'm not suggested it's likely to amass 10 million, John was unusual. But, it's not impossible to amass 1 million. And who would imagine that *New Yorker* Magazine copy editor, Lu Burke would leave a million dollar legacy to her favorite library?[2] The rich are all around, but difficult to pick out of a crowd. Don't be surprised on your visit to Wal-Mart or Costco if there are a few millionaires undetected in the store.

Although a ten million dollar estate is unusual, retiring with one million dollars is not impossible if you start saving early and contribute to your investment account regularly. But, it won't happen if you live extravagantly now!

THIS SOUNDS TOO HARD

When you are starting out, your finances are tight and it's crucial to deliberately decide how to allocate your income. How you spend directly impacts how wealthy you will become.

The spending section is intentionally placed after the Debt and Saving Sections because getting rid of debt and saving are crucial to getting rich.

> Learn to adjust your spending to the amount
> of your accessible cash. Take out the debt payments
> and savings first! Spend what you have left.

If you're not left with much cash, then figure out ways to live on the money you have or make more money.

There is no secret. If you overspend now, you destine your future to financial pain. What would you say if I told you you'll make at least four million dollars by age 65? Sound impossible? It's not!

Assume you're a 23 year old college graduate making the average salary of $46,000. With 3 percent raises each year, at age 65 you'll have earned about four million dollars. If you are an ambitious individual and bulk up your salary and raises, you will earn significantly more over your working lifetime.

Do you think you could adjust your spending a bit and invest some of those earnings? If you do, they will grow into a substantial nest egg. It's possible to earn the average salary your entire life, invest smartly, and at retirement have a million dollars saved up. All of this while making a few simple spending, saving, and investing choices.

The difference between a comfortable retirement and insufficient funds at age 65 are smart lifestyle and investing choices.

SPENDING CHOICES

We live in a beautiful, immaculately maintained condominium community. We own our condominium and pay a small monthly fee for outside maintenance for the common areas and pool. Since we purchased our home with a fixed rate mortgage, loan payments will never increase. Our salaries may go up, but not our mortgage payment. As our income increases, our mortgage payment becomes a smaller percent of our income.

Abutting our middle class condominium complex is an exclusive rental community. The rents on some larger units rival our monthly mortgage payment. However, this section is not about whether to buy or rent...it is about spending choices.

In an unscientific survey, I compared the automobiles in the condominium parking lot with those parked in the apartment complex. The apartment complex garage housed more luxury vehicles than did the condominium parking lots. Most of the condominium owners own their own homes and are paying a monthly amount towards the payment of their mortgages. At a later date, these folks will own their homes outright. Whereas, the renters are paying a monthly amount to the apartment owner and will never own their apartment. Furthermore, the apartment dwellers live in a luxury complex and may never save the amount necessary to purchase their own home. With luxury cars galore in the apartment complex parking lot, these folks are spending a few hundred bucks extra for their expensive cars, further depleting their resources and decreasing the amount of money available for saving and investing.

If you pay $2,000 per month rent, and another $500 per month for a car note, in one year $30,000 is gone before you spend on groceries, gas, insurance, or any other day to day living expenses.

The point is simple, live rich now, with a fancy car and luxury apartment, and miss the opportunity for long term wealth.

Adjust spending patterns a bit, and see how you can become rich. If I told you that by cutting back your rent and car payments, you could afford to buy a home within five years, would you be interested?

Take on a roommate or two, and move to a more affordable apartment. Those two spending choices could cut your rent payments to $700 per month. Buy a more affordable car and slice your auto payments in half. Make these two lifestyle changes and free up $1,550 per month.

Divert that $1,550 per month savings into an investing account funded with a broad based stock index fund with an average annualized 7 percent return. (Be aware that investment returns go up and down, and your return may be less than projected.) At the end of five years, your money could grow to $110,969. That's more than enough to put down on a new home or condominium with money to spare.

Spending decisions directly
impact future lifestyle choices.

Lifestyle choices create your today and your future. If you want to be fat and unhealthy, then don't exercise or worry about what you eat. The same goes for money. If you want to be poor at retirement, lack funds for emergency expenses, live in an apartment your entire life, then spend all of your money now and don't think about the future! If your get rich plan is buying lottery tickets, prepare to rely on Social Security in retirement.

SKIP THE BUDGET

If you lack the patience to track your spending and make a budget? There is another way.

For non-budgeters, here is how to spend.

Deduct savings automatically as recommended in *"Step 2: Saving-The Path to More Benjamins"*.

Spend the remaining money on essentials first and leisure activities last:

- Rent and utilities
- Food
- Daycare and child related expenses
- Insurance
- Transportation
- Clothing
- Recreation and entertainment
- Miscellaneous

This strategy is simple and it works. Since you've already made your debt payments and transferred money for saving and investing, the rest is yours to use. If there's not enough left, figure out how to adjust your expenses. Regardless, you can be confident your money is growing and providing a financial cushion for now and the future.

You just learned the simplest spending strategy ever; you can stop reading here, and skip to the next chapter, or learn to budget.

HOW TO BUDGET

You do not have to budget! But, creating and maintaining a budget can jump start your get rich plan.

Budgeting helps track where your money is going and is useful for long term planning. When you track spending, you actually see where your money is going and you can evaluate which spending categories to adjust. In fact, seeing where your money goes is frequently enough motivation for you to adjust spending.

Wander the aisles at The Quickmart; grab a coke, granola bar and pack of gum. Without a budget, you don't think much about the $5.00 spent on your snack. You'll think twice about shelling out the cash if you record every cent you spend. The five bucks a day add up to more than $1,500 in a year!

The goal of budgeting is to spend on things that give you the greatest amount of value.

I've kept a family budget on Quicken for many years. One of the reports compares the budgeted amount with the actual amount spent on each category. One month I noticed that although we budgeted $150 for the family to eat out, the review turned up $250 spent on restaurant meals for that month. The $100 increase in restaurant expenses stared me in the face; I couldn't ignore the numbers. It was a no-brainer, we needed to cut back on restaurant visits the next month. Restaurant meals are an easy category to run up the bills and to cut back. And there are many more discretionary places to reign in the spending.

Awareness is the starting point for habit change.

USE A SPENDING CHART

For one month keep track of spending.

- Take a notebook with you everywhere and jot down what you spend in the notebook for a month.

- Or, use your mobile as a notepad or find an APP to download and track spending.

At the end of the month, use your spending log to:

- Create Target Spending/Saving amounts in *Target Amount* column.

- At the end of the month. Calculate the *Difference*.

- Adjust target amounts for the following month.

Use this simple chart as a guide:

Barbara Friedberg Personal Finance © Spending Chart			
MONTH:	Target Amount	Actual Amount	Difference
SAVING/INVESTING			
DEBT PAYMENTS			
RENT/MORTGAGE			
UTILITIES-gas & electric			
PHONE			
INTERNET			
TRANSPORTATION			
FOOD AT HOME			
FOOD OUT			
ENTERTAINMENT			
CLOTHES			
INSURANCE			
PERSONAL CARE			
CHILD CARE			
HOUSEHOLD			
MISCELLANEOUS			
TOTAL			

Keep track simply. Another alternative is an online budgeting tool. Sometimes the simplest tools are the best. Do what works for you. It's surprising, but the act of tracking your spending has an unusual impact; you end up spending less. By writing down the expenses, impulse spending declines and you're automatically creating a pause button.

Any habit change is difficult. Try it for a week and see what happens. Does a week seem overwhelming? Try tracking your spending for a day or two. Start small and strengthen your spending monitor muscle.

DON'T HAVE ENOUGH LEFT AFTER DEBT AND SAVINGS PAYMENTS?

It's not unusual to have more month than money. In fact, it's the norm. After debt payments and saving, what if there's not enough money left for your current lifestyle? You'll be surprised at how some people have learned to thrive, while creatively managing their spending.

HOW TO MODIFY YOUR SPENDING

Get in the habit of uncovering less expensive spending alternatives. Make small adjustments in your lifestyle to create wealth.

- Rent too much? Get a roommate or two (or three?).
- Food costs too high? Choose lower cost substitutes. Beans and rice anyone? How about another peanut butter and jelly for lunch? A famous chef disclosed that he eats Ramen noodles at home. At $1.00 a pouch, you have a great meal substitute.
- No money for clothes? Shop sales, thrifts stores, and outlets stores. Swap with friends. Take care of the clothing you have. Combine entertainment with saving and host a clothes swap party with friends.
- No money for fun? Host a potluck in your apartment.
- Check the internet for low cost fun activities. Hello happy hour; nurse a drink and nibble on free hors d'oeuvres.

- For any larger purchase, designate a 24-48 hour waiting period before you buy. Second thoughts can adjust your "needs."

- Buy special occasion clothes at the consignment shop, or rent that party dress. For the best stuff, visit the thrift stores near expensive neighborhoods.

- If you live in a big city, consider losing the car and rent or ride sharing when you need a vehicle.

- Develop smart spending habits now; skip the $3.00 coffee and brew at home, bring your lunch, and drink water instead of soda with a restaurant meal.

- Over a lifetime, you will save thousands of dollars.

> It's easier to cut expenses than to earn more.

There are some who say these small changes aren't the answer and earning more is the way to amass great wealth. The problem with this thinking is that no matter how much you earn, you can always spend more than you earn. Regardless of your income level, if you don't save, and invest a portion of your earnings, you will never be wealthy.

The Institute for Financial Literacy's 2010 Annual Consumer Bankruptcy Demographics Report[1] found that almost 60 percent of those who went bankrupt had at least some college education, with degree holders at almost 30 percent. Although concentrated among lower income folks, 9.18 percent of those bankruptcy filers in 2010 earned over $60,000 per year. Clearly, a higher income does not prevent bankruptcy.

Find a few extra bucks every day with smart spending choices, bank the savings, and your wealth will grow.

Before we go on, I can hear the whining. This is too hard; I'm not having any fun. I don't have enough money to live on. I can't do this.

Okay, maybe you can't cut back as much as you'd like now; don't quit.

Start small and make a tiny change. Have a vegetarian meal one night a week. Skip the temptation at the mall this month. Eat a snack at home before meeting your friends at a restaurant, and then order a bowl of soup for your meal!

Crystal, from Budgeting in the Fun Stuff dot com, used this approach:

> "When my husband and I graduated from college, we continued to live cheap, like dirt poor, for two years even though we had good jobs. The excess income is fantastic if you want to pay off debt or save for a big goal like a house down payment. We ended up buying our home when we were just 23."

Try thinking before you buy.

Practice mindful spending and pay attention to your spending decisions. Remember, little expenses matter and turn into lifetime money drains.

The more you spend now, the less you will have later.

Step 4:
Get A Cool Crib Cheap

"The ache for home lives in all of us, the safe place where we can go as we are and not be questioned."

Maya Angelou

A comfortable home environment makes your life richer. You do not need a fancy place or a large palace, rather you need a space that is yours and is within your budget. When you get your home space in order, the rest of your life will be smoother.

REAL ESTATE STREET CRED

I am addicted to HGTV. I know every host and have seen most episodes of every show on the network. Well... maybe not all of the "International House Hunters" episodes. Top that off with the fact that I've worked in and been around the real estate industry my entire life.

My husband and I lived in nine apartments, condominiums, or homes. Before marriage, I went from my folk's home to college dorms, communal living, and three apartments where I lived alone. All told, I've lived in most housing situations available in the United States and twice in Spain.

The housing goal is to maximize your living situation and minimize the cost. Before you search for an apartment or home, do a quick self-checkup. Use the upcoming Housing

Decision Chart© or come up with your own method. Figure out what you are willing to compromise and your "must haves." The funny thing is, no matter your budget, there are always trade-offs.

One of my favorite HGTV shows is "Selling New York." The real estate in that region rivals the most expensive in the country and few New York real estate buyers appear with a budget south of one million dollars. You would think that with access to $1,000,000 or more the buyers could get whatever they want. Actually, the high priced homes require sacrifices just like those necessary for a buyer with a budget of $150,000. I'm shocked that many multimillion dollar apartments have old kitchens and tiny powder rooms. Who wants to buy a million dollar home and then have to remodel? If million dollar home buyers have to compromise be assured that you will too.

RENT VERSUS BUY

Are you cut out to be a home owner? Are you ready to take on the ongoing maintenance and repairs of a home in lieu of calling the manager to unclog the drain? It's on you when the interior needs repainting, the microwave goes out, and the grass needs mowing. When a pipe bursts on a Saturday night in the cold of winter, it's your responsibility to call a plumber and pay him time and a half for showing up on the week-end. That's the negative side of owning versus renting.

Renters call the landlord to fix the burst pipes and a broken microwave. That's the easy part. On the down side, as the rent increases, you either pay up or move to another place, where the rent will eventually increase as well.

Renters have the benefit of turning repairs and

maintenance over to the landlord, but don't have a chance to build up equity in real estate and eventually own their home. Owning real estate is an excellent way to get rich over the long term. Consider renting for a time while you save money to purchase a home.

Keep rent costs low and add a roommate or two to save money. If you would like to own real estate, be willing to change some of your "must haves" into preferences. Do you really need the granite countertops now? Carlos and Liz, a young married couple lived with two students in a two bedroom rental in order to save up for a down payment.

There isn't a perfect housing decision. You decide whether to rent or buy based on your personal circumstances. Matthew and his wife do not want to buy because they liked the flexibility that renting offered. As you rank your preferences systematically it's easier to make your housing decision.

RANK YOUR WANTS

Shannon Sharpe, the hall of fame tight end football player and his equally talented brother, Sterling, grew up in Glenville, Georgia, in a cinderblock home with no running water or indoor plumbing. The bathroom was in the woods out back. They didn't realize they were dirt poor because that was the only life they knew. Yet, as they aged, the Sharpe brothers hungered for more. History tells the rags to riches story of these two successful and tenacious men.

The Sharpe brothers are examples of the many lower income individuals who achieved success from humble backgrounds. Their story highlights the distinction between wants and needs. What you need is fairly simple; a roof over your head, indoor plumbing, and heat. The Sharpe brothers grew up with no indoor plumbing and achieved great success. It's helpful to grasp that many of your perceived "must haves" are preferences. Your future wealth and success are not determined and may be hindered by a luxury home.

Don't believe you need granite countertops and a spa tub. Every apartment, condominium, or home you preview will fulfill your basic needs with running water, indoor plumbing, a kitchen, bathroom and living space. Your needs will be filled. Once you realize that everything else is a choice you can prioritize your wants, according to your own preferences. Be mindful that every luxury you buy in your twenties and thirties sacrifices future wealth. Spend wisely to enjoy life now and build for the future.

Complete this Housing Decision Chart and prioritize your wants.

Barbara Friedberg Personal Finance HOUSING DECISION CHART© Rank your housing preferences from 1 – 10 (1=least important; 10=most important)		
TYPE OF HOUSING	**RANK**	**NOTES**
Buy single family home		
Rent single family home		
Buy condominium		
Rent apartment		
Rent a room		
ALONE OR ROOMMATES		
I want to live alone		
I wouldn't mind a roommate		
I'm willing to live with multiple roommates		

PREFERENCES		
City setting		
Suburban setting		
Near public transportation		
Modern building		
Older building		
Pool		
Workout facility		
Laundry in building		
Air conditioned		
Yard or outdoor space		
Deck or balcony		
Parking garage or space		
Location:		
	MINIMUM	MAXIMUM
PRICE RANGE		
SUMMARY		

Differentiate your wants and preferences from your needs. Ask yourself if you're willing to give up some luxury now to ensure a wealthy future later. When choosing how to live consider commuting costs, condominium fees, utilities, and extras that may not be readily apparent. Then, talk your decision over with a trusted friend, partner, or parent as spending wisely on housing now can accelerate your wealth later.

HOUSING TIPS OVERVIEW

With your preferences outlined, check the rental or housing market. Look online and visit a few places to see if your budget supports your wish list. If not, revise and reconsider. Winnow your "must haves" list to those true essentials and consider additional locations, types of housing, or roommates to increase your options and lower your costs.

One of my favorite apartments was a one room studio in a large old house. The bedroom, dining, and living room were one large room with a small kitchen on one side and a bathroom on the other. It was a perfect solution for one person and the rent was cheap.

Don't get hung up on things you can change; décor, window coverings, and furnishings can turn the plainest space into a dramatic home.

When roommates are involved, be sure to do some screening of your own. Ask potential roomies basic questions to get a feel for their living style and financial situation. If you are renting together, make sure you set up rules in advance, and get the roommate on the lease.

One of my earlier roommates, Betsy, didn't pay her share of the rent. Next, I asked Betsy to move out. When she didn't comply, I finally moved her stuff out of the apartment and into the front yard. This experience taught me an important lesson; I should have screened her before choosing to live with Betsy.

When you are ready to commit, realize that every price is

negotiable. Don't write off places a bit north of your budget; it's worth a shot to see if the landlord or seller will work with you on price, updates, or other items. If the price is okay, but the interior could use some paint or updated carpet, don't be afraid to ask. Although you want a place to live, don't forget that the landlord wants a reliable tenant. Unless you are in a highly competitive rental market, do not be afraid to walk away.

A train conductor taught me the power of walking away during a negotiation.[1] I overheard the conductor telling his associate how he set the rental price he could afford. The train conductor visited apartments and if the potential landlord would not meet his price, he walked away. He did not haggle. At a beautiful apartment, as the conductor walked away after stating his price, the rental agent ran after him and agreed to the price. Sometimes, the simple act of walking away will cause the landlord to meet your terms. If not, find someplace else within your financial parameters.

Don't forget to watch your online profile. Eliminate the Facebook pictures showing you in a trashed room drunk on the floor. This is not a good message to send a potential landlord or home seller. If renting is your preference, use the following strategies to snare the most apartment for your money.

IS RENTING FOR YOU?

If you decide to rent, follow these steps to get a nice place, for an affordable rent payment.

3 STEPS TO RENT AN APARTMENT

1. Prepare

Gather documents that support your ability to pay the rent; paycheck stubs, verification of current employment, and an employment history.

Prepare a references document which includes your name, home and email addresses, and phone number as well as a rental history with contact information. Include the name and contact information of your current employer who can vouch for your income.

Check your credit history at annualcreditreport.com. It's free! If you have credit problems, be prepared to counteract the landlord's concerns with assurances of how your current income is sufficient to cover the rent payment. Bring justification and proof of recent on-time service, credit card, or merchant payments. This helps verify that you're a good risk for the landlord and will pay the rent on time.

2. Scout Apartments

To find vacancies, visit Craigslist, newspaper classified, ask friends, and tour neighborhoods of interest.

View potential apartments. Jot down likes, dislikes, and damages. Don't forget to take pictures to review later.

When you decide on an apartment, let the property owner know you're interested. If you have good credit and rental history, check out comparable area rents and consider negotiating a lower payment or extras (parking, storage, washer/dryer). As we've discussed previously, everything is negotiable.

3. Sign the Lease

Read the entire lease before signing. If you're unsure of anything, have a lawyer look it over. Do not sign without a complete understanding of the terms.

Walk through the apartment immediately after signing to check for damage, and if found, contact the owner right away. If you don't inform the landlord of prior damage, you may be charged for damage you didn't create.

WHAT NOT TO DO WHEN RENTING

We live in a condominium next door to a luxury apartment complex. The 3 bedroom apartments rent for $2,600 per month. Porsche's, BMW's, and Lexus' populate the parking lot. Some apartment dwellers pay $2,600 rent and $650 car payments per month. After one year, what does the renter have to show for her $39,000? At the end of one year, the renters' dropped almost $40,000 on rent and car payments, with no home equity built up and a car with depreciating value. If those are deliberate decisions, reflective of the renter's values and choices, that's fine. But it's important to recognize the tradeoffs of spending now, without attention to saving for the future.

The next section maps out how alternate choices can put you in a home, building equity, instead of a lifelong renter.

RENT TO OWN AND SAVE $ 50,000

I understand some folks want to drive a luxury car. My mom and dad did! I also appreciate the desire to live in a nice place.

But renting an expensive apartment and driving a premium

car does not lead to long term wealth unless you are also putting money away for the future.

Watch how the renters above could adjust their spending, tweak their lifestyle and save $50,000 in three years.

BEFORE		AFTER	
Rent 3 bedroom apartment	$2,600 per month	Rent 2 bedroom apartment	$1,500 per month
New luxury car	$650 per month	3 year old BMW (48,000 miles- cost $23,400- financed $20,000 for 4 years at 3.5%)	$447 per month

Cut costs for three years and go from spending $3,250 for rent and car to $1,947 per month. That's a savings of $1,303 per month. Sock away that $1,303 per month and at the end of three years you save $46,908.

Is it worth cutting back to get rich? That's an example of how to curb your wants in order to get rich. In fact the wealthy and successful businessman, Mark Cuban[2] recommends;

> "Save your money. Save as much money as you possibly can. Every penny you can. Instead of coffee, drink water. Instead of going to McDonald's, eat mac and cheese. Cut up your credit cards. If you use a credit card, you don't want to be rich. The first step to getting rich requires discipline. If you really want to be rich, you need to find the discipline, can you?"

BUYING A HOME

Home owners build ownership equity in their home, and eventually own their home free and clear. Add that benefit to the reality of taking out a fixed mortgage, where your payments remain constant throughout the life of the loan and you control a majority of your housing expense. A $1,600 mortgage payment may seem like a bundle now, but with inflation and a growing income, in several years the payment will be a smaller percent of your take home pay. Contrast that with rising rent payments over which you have no control.

If you decide to buy, it's much easier in a lower cost of living area. In many parts of the country a home or condominium can be had for $150,000 or less. In Chicago, New York, San Francisco, and the largest cities across the country, you'll pay many times that amount for a starter home.

If you live in a pricey area and are having difficulty saving for a down payment, you may want to consider relocating. A three bedroom, two bathroom, home in San Francisco costs $1,000,000 or more. If you move to Atlanta, a similar home can be purchased for $200,000. Obviously, relocating is a major decision, yet, owning a home and building equity is easier in lower cost of living areas.

My husband and I began our careers in San Diego, and moved to the Midwest to raise our family. Now that our daughter is grown, and we've enjoyed the benefits of appreciating home ownership, we've returned to the more expensive California.

When buying, it's preferable to have 10 to 20 percent of the purchase price for a down payment and borrow the remainder with a real estate mortgage. Although, if you lack a large down payment, the Federal Housing Authority

(FHA) has programs that only require a small down payment. In a lower cost of living area, saving fifteen to twenty thousand dollars might be possible in several years of extreme saving. In higher cost of living areas, it will take longer. Once you're in your own home, you can always take in a renter to help defray the mortgage costs.

One final caution, do not stretch your budget for housing. You decide how much you can afford. The lender doesn't understand your financial obligations and preferences. The landlord doesn't care if you're paying 30 percent or more of your take home pay for rent. You'll thwart future money pressures and buy or rent less home than you can afford. Be conservative in your choice and understand that this is likely one of many future homes you will inhabit.

Step 5:
Stuff Happens-Protect Yourself From Loss

"I don't want to tell you how much insurance I carry with the Prudential, but all I can say is: when I go, they go too."

Jack Benny

You may not need as much life insurance as the legendary funny man Jack Benny (ask your grandparents about him), but if you have a car, an apartment, a body; then you need insurance.

Stuff happens. No matter where you live, apartments get robbed. If you have valuables, you need renters insurance. If everything you own is junk and you can afford to replace it, you can skip the renters insurance.

Imagine this: it's midnight in your cozy first floor apartment. The window is cracked on the warm summer night. You're sleeping like a baby when you hear a rustling sound, which sounds like a window opening. Just as you crack open your eyes, there is a man climbing in your window, stepping on the dresser and then on to the bed. Panic strikes, you feign sleep, grab the phone, and punch in 911 as the intruder runs out the bedroom and into the living room.

This happened to my husband and me.

On the way out, the burglar grabbed my laptop, television,

engagement ring, and wallet. The total loss was almost $4,000.

That's why you need insurance.

Burglaries are very common. In fact, if you live in a big city, you can count on being robbed at some time. Certainly, having insurance won't keep you from being robbed, but it will replace the losses you incur.

YOU CAN'T CONTROL EVERYTHING

Insurance is for the events in life you can't control. Purchase insurance, not for the small stuff, but for that $10,000 catastrophic medical or car repair expense. Your chance of being in an auto accident is great. In fact, do you know any driver who has not had a fender bender?

The Affordable Care Act makes health insurance more affordable and there are subsidies to help cover the costs.

Under the Affordable Care Act, if you lack health insurance, you're subject to fines. And that's not the worst outcome. If you rack up huge medical bills, without insurance, you're liable for the tab. If you don't pay up, your bank account can be seized, wages garnished, and liens may be placed on your property (depending upon your state of residence). Of course, this situation will also devastate your credit.

In other words, you are liable for the debt. And the hospital has a variety of legal means to collect their debt which includes taking money from your bank account and paycheck.

This same scenario can play out in other insurable areas of your life.

I understand that it's difficult and unpleasant to pay insurance premiums for occurrences which may never happen. But if these unforeseen catastrophes happen and you don't have insurance, your life can be devastated. That's why they call it "insurance."

> Buying insurance doesn't increase wealth,
> but lack of insurance can destroy it.

WHAT IS THIS #?*$% INSURANCE LANGUAGE?

I was baffled by "insurance terms". It took a while to understand what the strange words such as "premium" and "insured" meant. Is a premium a prize for purchasing insurance? It sounds nice doesn't it? To simplify the jargon, here's a glossary of insurance words:

Insurance: Financial reimbursement when disaster strikes. Buy auto insurance and after a car wreck you get money from the insurance company to repair the damage.

Insurer: That's the insurance company.

Insured: That's you, the individual covered by the insurance policy.

Policy: The name of the insurance agreement or contract between you and the insurance company.

Premium: The amount the insurance company charges to purchase the insurance policy. It's a bill, not a prize.

Policyholder: The person who buys and owns the insurance policy.

Deductible: When disaster hits, this is the amount you agree to pay before the insurance company reimbursement is made. Decide whether to pay $250, $500, or $1,000 of the claim. Hint: choose a higher deductible if you can afford it to reduce your insurance premium.

Claim: A request to the insurance company for reimbursement for a loss. For example, you hit a pole while driving and it costs $1,000 to repair the vehicle. Pay the first $250 (your deductible) and file a claim with the insurance company to receive the remaining $750 in repair expenses.

WHAT TYPE OF INSURANCE TO GET

Insurance companies offer life insurance for a one year old baby, insurance to pay your mortgage if you die, insurance to pay for a change in travel plans and many more varieties. Do not insure events that are inexpensive to cover on your own, or are paid for by other coverage. Do you need insurance to pay for your mortgage due to death or disability? Not if you have life or disability insurance. Can you afford a $150 charge if you need to reschedule an airline flight? If so, you don't need travelers insurance.

Consider the big events and insure against those. Forget about the rest.

Renters insurance: If you own decent furniture and clothing which is expensive to replace in the event of a theft or fire, then pick up renter's insurance. It's cheap, and costs about $16 per month depending upon the amount of coverage you get and where you live. Make sure to keep a record of your belongings, so if you get robbed, you can document what was stolen.

Home owners insurance: If you own a home or condo, insurance is required by the mortgage lender. To lower the premiums keep the deductible as high as possible.

Health insurance: It's crucial (and required by law under the Affordable Care Act) to be covered by health insurance. If you're under 26, stay on your parents' policy. Those over 26, can get health insurance through an employer or the government healthcare marketplace (https://www.health care.gov/marketplace/). Be sure to investigate your state's health insurance website as well. The self- employed can check out the government marketplace and small business associations and other professional memberships for a group plan.

Disability insurance: Often overlooked, this type of coverage pays cash when an accident or illness prevents you from working.

Are you over age 35? Your chance of losing the ability to work for ninety days or more due to illness or injury is greater than your chances of dying.[1] Even younger workers get injured and need short term cash to cover expenses while they're out of commission. Fortunately, many employers offer disability insurance.

Vehicle insurance: Just about every U.S. state requires vehicle insurance. Shop around for the best price. Don't forget mom and dad's company, they might have special prices for you. Always ask about discounts for which you may qualify.

Term life insurance: Get this if you have kids or someone depending on your income like a spouse. Term is economical life insurance without any unnecessary extras. If you're not married and don't have anyone depending on your income for their survival, skip life insurance. There are those that will try and tell you to get life insurance if you have no dependents. Think about it. Why do you need life insurance if your death won't result in financial hardship for someone else?

DO YOU NEED WHOLE LIFE INSURANCE?

Insurance agents may encourage you to buy "whole life insurance." The standard pitch is that you get an investment product combined with life insurance. Don't go for it. Don't mix your investing and insurance. It's cheaper and more prudent to keep these two purchases separate. Insurance is protection against loss. Investing is a strategy for wealth generation. Don't combine the two.

INSURANCE TIPS:

- Insurance is a commodity, which means that there's not much difference between the identical coverage purchased from different vendors.

- Shop around for the best price. Commit an hour or two of research on line and save hundreds of dollars.

- Check your associations (church, alumni, or professional association) for special group rates.

- Bundle all of your insurance with one company to save money.

- Ask about discounts. There are always discounts such as a good driving record, or living near a fire hydrant that can lower your premiums.

- If you have some cash in an emergency fund, choose a higher deductible to lower your premiums.

- Before buying a vehicle, check out the cost to insure. You might be surprised at how the age, make and model impact premium prices.

- Do not smoke. Smoking increases all four insurance rates. And it kills you before your time!

- If you're buying insurance from an unfamiliar company, check out their rating on AM Best to make sure they are rated highly.

Bite the bullet and get the insurance you need. Don't over insure against possible loss, but figure out a reasonable amount of coverage in each area. Frequently, your employer will offer health insurance. Look at the options and choose the plan that best fits your needs. Go through the remaining categories, check some online insurers and buy the coverage. Then, every few years, review your insurance premiums to determine whether they continue to offer the coverage you need for the best value.

Step 6:
Be A Portfolio Player!
I Have No Money
Investing Strategy

"Investing should be more like watching paint dry or watching grass grow. If you want excitement, take $800 and go to Las Vegas."

Paul Samuelson

I can hear the complaining, "You expect me to save for a rainy day, pay my bills, get insurance, and have money for investing?"

Before you tune out, look at the evidence. It's easier to invest and get rich than you think.

Jack and Jill were busy getting their careers going, and investing was the last thing on their minds. Read about how one decision turned into hundreds of thousands of dollars.

JILL'S STORY

At age 25, Jill got a notice from the human resources department telling her how easy it was to invest in the company's retirement plan. Furthermore, if she did, her company would match part of her contribution with free money from the company. She trotted up to the personnel office, and arranged to have $200 per month deducted from her salary and directed to two stock index mutual funds and a bond index mutual fund.

Each month Jill invested $200 per month and her company added another $100, bringing the total up to $300 per month.

She invested the monthly retirement money this way:

- 40% ($120) in Vanguard Total Stock Market Index Fund (VTSMX)
- 30% ($90) in Vanguard International Stock Index Fund (VTIAX)
- 30% ($90) in Vanguard Total Bond Market Index Fund (VTBLX)

She started investing at age 25 and stopped at age 65, for a total of forty years.

At age 65, Jill's contributions plus the employers' grew to $787,444[1].

JACK'S STORY

Jack wasn't so smart. He avoided thinking about investing. Jack threw the unopened retirement plan information into the trash.

At age 40, Jack woke up one morning and realized that he had no money invested for his future and Jack was scared. He started investing and chose the same investments as Jill. In an attempt to catch up, Jack invested $400 per month, twice as much as Jill's $200.

Jack's employer matched his $400 per month with an additional $100, just like Jill's employer.

At age 65, Jack's contribution plus the employers' grew to $405,036, while Jill's lesser contributions grew to almost twice that amount at $787,444.

	Jack & Jill total Contributions	Employer's Contributions	Combined Total Contributions	Portfolio Value at Age 65
JILL	$96,000	$48,000	$144,000	$787,444
JACK	$120,000	$30,000	$150,000	$405,036

Jack invested $24,000 more than Jill and ended up with $382,408 less than Jill.

Jill invested less money than Jack, how did she end up with more money at age 65 than he did?

Simple, Jill started earlier. Jill had the benefit of compounded returns over time.

Over time, it is neither exceptionally painful nor difficult to amass large sums of money, if you start early enough. Unfortunately, the later you begin investing, the less time your investment dollars have to compound. That is why there is urgency in your twenties and thirties to start investing for retirement.

QUICK PRIMER ON STOCKS, BONDS, AND MUTUAL FUNDS

Serena, an old friend, recently recounted an evening at a high pressure investment seminar. She said the presenters mentioned something about a real estate trust. The speakers touted the wonderful properties of this investment vehicle. She had no clue what the investment was or what the presenter was saying. All she understood was that the speaker wanted her to buy this "great investment" and she was certain to get a big fat return. Does that sound like enough information to you?

You must understand your investments. It is straightforward to understand investing basics. When exercising to become fit, you don't need to become proficient in mixed martial arts. A $10 set of weights and some running shoes will suffice. Lift the weights, walk, or run four or five days per week and you're fit.

You don't need to become an investing genius to build wealth. In fact, many professionals fail to beat the unmanaged returns of stock market index funds. If you learn the properties of stocks, bonds, and index mutual funds, then you know enough. Ignore the blaring noise of the financial television pundits and the pricey financial advisors.

Don't worry about all the different types of investments out there. And if someone tries to sell you a "can't miss" opportunity, run quickly and don't look back. Understand index mutual funds and you're on your way to understanding the best investments available.

Stock: Part ownership in a corporation.
When the company profits, so do you.

Bond: Loan to a company or government for a specific time period in exchange for interest (coupon) payments.

Mutual Fund: A company that bundles groups of stocks and or bonds and sells them to investors. Buy a slice of the mutual fund and you own a tiny portion of many stocks and/or bonds.

> Index Fund: A type of mutual fund that buys a diversified group of stocks or bonds, similar to those in popular indexes such as the Standard & Poor's 500 (largest 500 US stocks). Diversified investing with low fees.
>
> Exchange Traded Fund (ETF): Bundles financial assets like a mutual fund, but can be bought and sold on the stock exchange for a commission and may sell at a premium or discount to net asset value

Although there are hundreds of index funds, ranging from the very narrow specific country fund, such as a China Fund, to the obscure international bond funds, most of those mutual funds will not significantly beat the returns of a portfolio comprised of a few broad based stock and bond funds. Jill invested in one stock index mutual fund comprised of U.S. companies and another with international companies. Her third index mutual fund held a variety of bonds.

Now, you know enough to select your index mutual funds. Look for low management fees, less than 0.50 percent and a mix of broadly diversified U.S.A. (or your home country) and international stock index funds. Add a widely diversified bond index fund and you're done.

COMPOUND INTEREST

"The most powerful force in the universe is compound interest," according to Albert Einstein.

Jack and Jill witnessed the magic of compound interest and the time value of money. Although a high return on your money is preferable, the most important contributor to wealth creation is time. There is no substitute for time invested.

Imagine investing just $2,400 per year (plus $1,200 per year contributed by the employer) during your working life and ending up with $787,440. What if Jill contributed even more? It's not as hard to amass wealth as one would think.

Simply put, compound interest is the manifestation of earning money on top of the money already invested. You make the initial investments and the force of compounding does the rest.

TAKE THIS QUIZ TO LEARN ABOUT COMPOUNDING

Barbara Friedberg Personal Finance **THE POWER OF COMPOUNDING QUIZ**© Choose either Option 1 or Option 2:		
	Yes	No
Option 1: Receive a lump sum payment of $100,000 at the end of one month.		
Option 2: Receive the total value of one penny doubling on the first day of the month and the resultant amount doubling every subsequent day until the end of the month. (For example, on day one you get one penny, on day 2 you get 2 pennies, on day 3 your wealth grows to 4 pennies on day 5 your money doubles to 8 pennies and so on doubling each day until the end of the month).		
SCORING; **If you chose option 1, on day 31 you have $100,000.** **If you chose option 2, on day 31 you would have $10,737,418.**		

Clearly, obtaining a 100 percent return on your money every day is quite unlikely or dare I say, impossible. Yet, the takeaway is that time and rate of return work together to build wealth. On day 19, your penny doubling on each prior day is worth, $2,621. Does it appear that after two and a half weeks and a return of just over $2,500 that you will reach $10,000,000 by the end of the month? Certainly not.

Yet, on day 26 your wealth has grown to over $335,000. Although $335,000 is a lot of money, it is still a far cry from the 10 million accrued by the end of the month. By day 28, you surpass $1,300,000. As you earn more and more return, the base upon which your investments are compounded grows. And that's how your money makes money.

But you need the two components; time and rate of return. The earlier you begin investing, the more time you have for your wealth to compound. Of course your money will not double every day, but the longer it is invested the more time there is to earn returns on top of your initial investment. With a balanced allocation of investments, if history is any guide, a solid rate of return is achievable.

ARE YOU READY TO BEGIN INVESTING?

The evidence is overwhelming that the earlier you start, the easier it is to amass wealth. Even though it is a struggle now, in the long run, your life will be much sweeter the earlier you begin investing. Your salary is likely to increase over time. Start early and as your income grows, you can invest a smaller percent of your total salary. That leaves more cash for consumption during your life.

Unless your salary is gigantic, living within your means and investing in your twenties and thirties requires sacrifice. Nevertheless, the alternative to beginning now versus later is greater sacrifice when you are older.

UNDERSTAND RISK AND REWARD IN INVESTING

Ever hear the phrase, "No pain, no gain?" In investing terms pain implies risk. The greater the potential return, the larger risk you must take. In reality, taking a large risk does not guarantee a large return, but a possibility of a large return. The flip side is that when you take a large risk, you also have the possibility of a large loss.

That sounds a bit scary; what if you don't want any risk and don't like the idea of your portfolio going up and down at all? In other words, it's kind of like saying, I don't want any unknowns in life at all. I want everything to be under my control. Sure, many of us prefer a smooth upward path in life, but that's impossible.

Read this quick overview of risk and reward in investing and then choose your own path.

Risk implies the possibility that your investment will lose money. In investing terms, that means the value of your investment dollars will fluctuate.

Here's a quick Investing 101 history lesson to arm you with basic long term investment returns information:

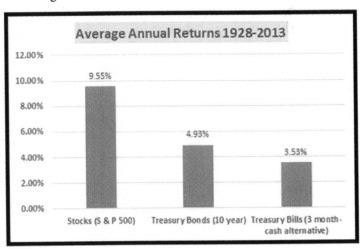

Average Annual Returns 1928-2013

Stocks (S & P 500)	9.55%
Treasury Bonds (10 year)	4.93%
Treasury Bills (3 month-cash alternative)	3.53%

Consider the outstanding overall long term results of investing in stocks for the last 85 years. Looks wonderful doesn't it? From 1928 to 2013 the US stock market averaged returns over 9 percent per year and bonds close to 5 percent. These averages mask the shorter term fluctuations imbedded into these returns.

Compare the historical returns with the more recent returns of 2002 through 2011.

Between 2002 and 2011, stock returns were 2.88 percent. These were extremely low stock market returns, in comparison with their historical long term returns. And Treasury bond returns from 2002 to 2011 were uncharacteristically high with 6.49 percent returns.

This data is more than perplexing, it is downright confusing. At the end of 2011, investors wondered if stocks would ever return to their historical averages and whether we were in a new normal of government bonds outperforming stocks.

With several years of outstanding stock market returns after 2011, the stock returns have rebounded.

Although the future is unknown, it is certain that stock and bond returns will go up and down. The best way to protect yourself financially and ensure you have enough money for your future necessities and dreams is to save and invest, starting now.

Since stock market returns are based on the growth of the underlying businesses; if you believe companies in the United States and abroad will continue to grow and expand, then you must keep a portion of your savings in stock investments to participate in that growth.

CHOOSE YOUR ASSET ALLOCATION

Asset allocation refers to the percent of investment dollars placed in various categories, such as stocks, bonds, and cash. Asset Allocation is the magic bullet of investing. Choose a variety of stocks, bonds, and cash investments to smooth out the risk of your investment portfolio and grow your wealth. (Some investors add in some real estate funds as well.)

When stocks go down in value, the cash and bond investments may hold steady or even go up. That creates smoother returns and helps protect your portfolio from drastic drops in value. Looking at historical returns, had you spread your investment monies across stocks and bonds, your returns would have been a combination of those assets and your asset values would have jumped around less than investing in stocks alone.

In general, bonds and cash are less risky than stocks. If you have less tolerance for volatility, put more of your investable assets in bonds and cash. In fact, a strategy recommended by Bodie and Taqqu in *Risk Less and Prosper* suggests you invest in Government I (inflation) Bonds and Treasury Inflation protected securities[2], to protect your basic future expenses from all volatility.

The more risk tolerant take an aggressive approach and put a greater percent in stock investments. That's because historically, stocks have returned more, but with greater volatility.

WHICH INVESTMENTS TO CHOOSE

Put your retirement money to work in a combination of these three types of mutual funds. Most plans offer a variation of similar stock and bond index funds. Choose the percent to include based on your personal risk tolerance. Invest more in bonds and cash if you prefer a less risky portfolio or are closer to retirement.

These are sample index funds. Your company's retirement plan or discount broker (if you are investing on your own) should offer similar funds. More sample index funds are listed in the appendix.

1. **Diversified U.S.A. Stock Index Fund;** for example, Vanguard Total Stock Market Index Fund (VTSMX)

2. **Diversified International Stock Index Fund;** for example, Vanguard Total International Stock Index Fund (VGTSX)

3. **Diversified Bond Index Fund;** for example, Vanguard Total Bond Market Index Fund (VTBLX)

For more detailed investment information download my free micro book, *How to Invest and Outperform Most Active Mutual Fund Managers*[3].

Investing when you are young is very important if you want a secure financial future. The simplest way to put the investing plan into action is the direct transfer from your paycheck. Have money transferred out of your paycheck and into a retirement account, you will not miss it.

The takeaway is to start immediately. How much you invest is less important than creating the habit to put money away for the future.

> You can increase the amount of savings as your income grows, but you cannot go back in time and start earlier.

Step 7:
Secrets Of The Rich

"If they had told me I was the janitor and would have to mop up and clean the toilets after the show in order to play, I probably would have done it."

Bruce Springsteen

For over 40 years, Springsteen dedicated himself to his passion, music. In the process, he's influenced millions of fans with stories of the real life trials and tribulations of ordinary people. Springsteen's wealth was accumulated over time. It's no coincidence that he would have mopped the floors in order to pursue his music. That dedication to a purpose can lead both to wealth and happiness.

You're worried about making ends meet, paying the bills, and keeping your job. With smart money habits, over time, your financial situation will improve. Many of the wealthy started out just like you, figuring out their place in life and learning to manage the multiple demands of balancing work, fun, spending, and saving. Learn their secrets. You may be surprised that most wealthy don't live rich.

Living "rich" leads to financial stress. Debt, excess consumption, and over focus on external appearances is detrimental to financial success, both now and in the future. Learn to want less and you will have more. A peek into the millionaire mind supports the idea that most wealthy individuals are not over consuming, brilliant, workaholics. In fact, their balanced lifestyle and diligent work habits make them difficult to identify.

Although money doesn't guarantee happiness, a certain amount solves stressful financial problems. As mentioned earlier, there is a base income of about $75,000 per year (data from 2010) which alleviates most financial worries. In addition, those earning more than that amount do not experience much additional life satisfaction.

Most young adults aren't earning $75,000.00, but consider the average income for folks your age. According to the National Center for Education Statistics1, the median salary for young adults with a bachelor's degree was $44,900. Just starting out, no spouse, no kids, no college costs, you don't need a huge salary to live, save, and invest. Cut out the excess indulgences and live in line with what's really important. If Mark Zuckerberg, the 28 year old billionaire founder of Facebook can show up in a hoodie and eat at McDonald's, do you really need to spend thousands on designer clothes and fine dining?

The rich do not live to impress. The wealthy are disciplined in their work habits. Many started working, saving, and investing at a young age. As underscored throughout the book, time and compound returns have an almost magical ability to create a secure retirement. Sensible spending, on items that you value, will leave enough for saving and investing.

Contrary to popular television shows, advertisements, and movies, the wealthy are not rushing to the mall on a whim, driving Porches, or jetting off to exotic locations every few months. Research backs up commonalities of the rich. In most cases, you cannot pick high net worth folks out in a crowd because they don't live to impress.

You will find the rich shopping at Wal-Mart just like you. The parking lot at our local store is filled with both luxury cars as well as the basic models. It's likely there are some rich bargain hunters packing the aisles along with low and middle income earners. Adjust your attitude and practice the habits of the wealthy so your financial woes are infrequent and short lived.

Thomas J. Stanley, bestselling author of *The Millionaire Next Door, The Millionaire Mind* and many other superbly researched studies of the wealthy, offers insight into the world of the rich. Culled from 733 survey respondents, the *Millionaire Mind* touted, "You cannot enjoy life if you are addicted to consumption and the use of credit."

The commonalities of the rich from Dr. Stanley's *Millionaire Mind* paint them as down to earth folks. The wealthy typically live in old established upper-middle-class neighborhoods, not trendy new developments. If you live in an exclusive apartment or home community and there's little cash left for other expenses; then you're living to impress, not for financial success. Contrary to popular belief, millionaires balance work with leisure. This supports the idea that you can become wealthy without being a workaholic. Millionaires are intelligent, not brilliant. Fortunately, you don't need to be a genius to achieve wealth. Finally, Stanley found his subjects practiced integrity, discipline, strong social skills, and hard work.

When my spouse and I were first married, we lived in sunny southern California. We loved the lifestyle, beach access, and climate. We didn't love the high cost of living that paid for the lifestyle. We both worked demanding schedules, my husband worked three part time jobs and I had a position at the local university. After commuting, there wasn't much time left to enjoy the San Diego paradise.

When our daughter was three, we made a difficult decision. We decided to trade the Southern California lifestyle for a more affordable one in the Midwest. We understood that moving to a lower cost of living area would give us more time as a family, the opportunity to live on one salary for a while, and build wealth for the future. The years spent in lower cost of living areas gave us financial and lifestyle benefits. We saved and invested more money at a younger age. That gave us a longer time to build wealth. In the affordable middle of the country, we could afford to live in better neighborhoods with top school districts. Those lifestyle decisions gave our daughter a great public school education.

Now that our daughter is an adult, we have the funds to live in a condominium in a more costly part of the country. The proximity to a vibrant big city and the ocean are wonderful lifestyle perks. We don't regret any past sacrifices to build our resources and reduce our living expenses. Over the years we had lots of fun, lived in great areas, vacationed, and still had funds to invest for the future. Had we remained in pricey Southern California our lifestyle would have been more expensive and hectic with less time and money left for recreation and investing.

THE WEALTHY DELAY GRATIFICATION

The wealthy understand that they cannot have everything they want immediately. The ability to delay gratification may be one of the most important traits of the affluent. Logically, if you buy whatever you want now, you have fewer resources available to buy a home later, fund your children's education, or retire comfortably. As reasonable as this sounds, there are countless people that avoid thinking about the future in order to justify overspending today.

Jordan had an awesome job in her early thirties. In addition to a six figure salary, her company gave her a Lexus. I was more than a bit jealous of her high income, fancy car, shopping sprees, and exotic vacations. At that same time, my spouse and I were struggling; living on one salary while we both took turns going to graduate school. A big night out for us was hitting the happy hour buffet at the local Mexican restaurant for cheap drinks and free hors d'oeuvres.

Over time, Jordan married and had a child. Their child enjoyed elite private schools and expensive summer camps.

Bloomingdales was their family department store and there were no visits to Target or Wal-Mart.

Like many others, Jordan had some financial setbacks. Yet, those setbacks didn't deter her spending. As she approaches retirement, she is stressed that her retirement funds are insufficient. Her salary has not kept up with its promising beginnings and she's worried about keeping her job. Her rent keeps rising as her salary stagnates. Jordan doesn't have enough money saved to retire comfortably. She spent rich her entire life, never bought a home, and approaches retirement with avoidable financial worries.

Save, invest, and spend smart now to lay the foundation for a solid financial life. The rich live and spend wisely. They aren't worried about keeping up with anyone nor having the newest, latest, or greatest gadgets. Follow the sensible lifestyles of the wealthy, do not fall prey to the lure of wasteful spending. Forget about TMZ's accounts of the latest reports from the Kardashian's, Lindsey Lohan, or the celebrity of the day. Those media hogs lifestyles should have no impact on your life, apart from entertainment.

According to *The Atlantic*, "Chart of the Day: 9% of American's are Millionaires in 2011"[2] most millionaires are not on television or in the media, but could be living next door.

The wealthy think before they spend.

ARE YOU ON THE PATH TO BECOME WEALTHY?

Take this quiz and find out.

Barbara Friedberg Personal Finance
WEALTH PREDICTOR QUIZ©

	Yes	No
Do you save at least 10 percent of your income?		
Are your housing expenses less than 30 percent of your net income?		
Do you wait and plan before making large purchases?		
Do you keep your vehicles for more than 8 to 9 years before replacing?		
Do you have an emergency fund in cash saved equal to 6 to 9 months of living expenses?		
Do you work more than 45-50 hours per week?		
Do you consider yourself frugal?		
Do you pay off your credit cards in full every month?		
Scoring; 1 point for every yes answer. 6 or more yes answers: You are on your way to becoming wealthy 3 or more no answers: If you want to become wealthy, reduce spending, and think before buying.		

Lifestyle decisions influence how much wealth you amass. How did you score on the "Wealth Predictor Quiz©"? Are you living a lifestyle which leads to wealth? Are you willing to tweak your spending and working life to get rich? It's not what you say, but how you act that determines how your life turns out.

If you scored low on this quiz, pause and decide if getting rich is really a priority. If so, then commit to changing your behaviors. Wishing will not make you rich. Working towards an objective leads to success. How you act and the choices you make, illustrate your priorities.

Have you ever met someone who speaks a good game? Danny spouts grand plans, goals, and wishes. Yet he never follows through. Danny has this money making scheme or that idea, but nothing ever comes to fruition. He doesn't follow through or take action. Like any other plan, you need to work to make it happen. Examine your behaviors. Are you taking actions to reach your aspirations? The rich take action to create wealth.

MORE EDUCATION EQUALS MORE MONEY

There are many paths to get rich, and the secret is choosing the path that fits with your interests. In spite of a poor market for new college graduates today, those with more education earn substantially more money over their working lives than those with less.

According to the Bureau of Labor Statistics more education is correlated with higher earnings and lower unemployment.[3]

In 2011, the median (half above and half below) weekly earnings by educational level was:

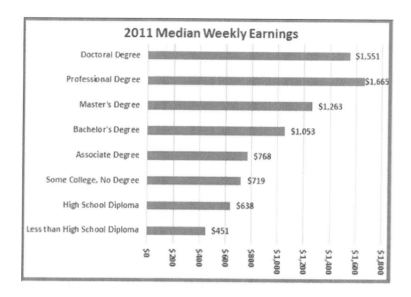

2011 Median Weekly Earnings

Degree	Earnings
Doctoral Degree	$1,551
Professional Degree	$1,665
Master's Degree	$1,263
Bachelor's Degree	$1,053
Associate Degree	$768
Some College, No Degree	$719
High School Diploma	$638
Less than High School Diploma	$451

GET HIGHER EDUCATION WITH LESS DEBT

Clearly, more education leads to higher wages. With the high cost of education, don't feel you must take on excessive debt to get an education. Go to community college for the first few years and transfer to a state university to keep costs down. Consider studying at an online university to further reduce educational expenses. Just make certain the university is accredited and well regarded.

You can choose to live like a pauper in college; remember it's only temporary. A bit of discipline and struggle will make you appreciate your greater earning power later.

My dad worked while going to college, studied while others were at the football games, and graduated with an engineering degree in 3 years. He's smart, not brilliant, but above all else, he's a hard worker.

Not only are those with more education higher earners but

they also experience less unemployment. Less education relates to greater unemployment. No one can take education away from you. Not only does education lead to greater wages over your lifetime, it makes you a wealthier and more knowledgeable individual. This leads to greater self-confidence and bestows an ability to think critically, handle adversity, and solve problems.

HOW WILL YOU GET RICH?

There are many paths to wealth. Some folks who amass a large nest egg never had extraordinary salaries. It's consoling to realize that you don't have to earn hundreds of thousands of dollars per year to become wealthy. In less than 30 years, you can amass one million dollars through investing. If you and your spouse each invest $600 per month, in 28.5 years, you could have a nest egg of one million bucks (assume you earn 6 percent per year annualized in a diversified portfolio of stock and bond index funds). If your employer adds to an investment account, all the money wouldn't even come out of your pocket.

Many millionaires start their own businesses to build wealth. Some of the most lucrative businesses are not glamorous. Consider running a few Subway franchises. Not afraid of a bit of manual labor? Why not start with one carpet cleaning business, and expand? Electricians, plumbers, and even barbers can become millionaires with the proper earning, spending, saving and investing paths. In fact, *The Wealthy Barber* by David Chilton tells his own rags to riches story, as a barber. Spend some time dreaming about the type of work you really enjoy. Is there a business opportunity behind your dreams?

Many professions offer large earning potential. With

initiative and persistence, sales of expensive items lead to large commissions. Successful realtors make thousands of dollars on one sale. Engineers and computer experts are in high demand and earn big salaries. That said, with disciplined lifestyle choices and saving, moderate earners can and do end up rich.

There is not one certain path to become wealthy. And for all but a rare few, the process of becoming rich is a long one. Don't be put off when you hit a roadblock.

Psychologists have long understood the importance of resilience in emotional wellbeing. In other words, those individuals who can pick themselves up after a loss, dust themselves off, and continue to work at a task or problem are the happiest. Not only are the resilient happier according to *Psychology Today*[4], but most highly successful individuals are also experienced at failure.

Charging ahead and overcoming obstacles is a requirement of the wealthy. No one gets a free pass from life's ups and downs. Yet those who get over the downs quickly are more likely to reach their goals. My dad has gotten sued, lost money, and been scammed by an employee. Yet, due to his relentless persistence, he overcame every obstacle in his path. From a life of poverty as a youth, he built not only financial wealth but also gave generously to othersSpend some time searching for your calling; it may not come on the first try. Do not get discouraged. Once you uncover the work that is fulfilling, begin immediately saving and investing. And look for additional ways to add to your funds. Many folks take on side jobs to build their next egg.

The secrets of the wealthy are that they're not very different from you and I. Link together smart money and lifestyle choices; delay gratification, put funds towards saving and investing regularly, work harder than most, and splurge less than the norm. Wealth is within your grasp. If getting rich is your goal, take a step today to make it a reality.

If you're rational, you understand the odds of winning the lottery are slight. Actually, your odds of getting hit by a lightning bolt and winning the lottery jackpot are about the same. On average, the lottery winner does win; about $.47 for every $1.00 spent.[5] Does that sound like a good money making strategy to you?

Step 8:
Short And Sweet Summary

"Every day I get up and look through the Forbes list of the richest people in America. If I'm not there, I go to work."

Robert Orben

Unless you are uber wealthy, you have to go to work. And if you are filthy rich, you don't need this book.

As Robert Orben the old comedy writer said, whether you like it or not, work is a reality.

It is never too late to create smart money habits and learn personal finance basics. Do not be surprised to uncover who amasses the greatest wealth over time, and it's not always those with the highest salaries.

In fact, 70 percent of lottery winners subsequently go bankrupt according to, "Financial planners: Winning the lottery isn't always a dream", by Deena Winter.[1] Wouldn't you expect that a lottery winner would be set for life? Not so. Having access to money does not ensure long term wealth.

Michael was a successful anesthesiologist living in beautiful San Francisco with his social worker wife and four children. He had a boat and an enviable lifestyle. For vacations they sailed the seas on their luxurious boat. Now Michael is in his late seventies and in deep financial trouble. He and his wife are living in Idaho in a two room cottage owned by his oldest daughter. They are constantly worried about money, would love to return to San Francisco and their boat. The boat is in shambles due to lack of upkeep and they cannot afford to return to California or to refurbish their boat.

What happened to land this successful doctor and his wife in deep financial trouble? They did not save much over their lives and assumed that they would work until their seventies. Michael had an accident at age 67 and can't work. They invested in several entrepreneurial ventures and real estate. Their real estate tanked in value during the recent economic downturn and their primary home was foreclosed upon. A deteriorating economy of 2006-2007 saw their businesses stumble and consume their savings.

If you make a few financial mistakes and learn from them you will be fine long term. But don't forget to save and maintain a cash cushion. That way, when a financial setback hits (and there's no avoiding it), you won't be forced to go into credit card debt or sell investments at an inopportune time.

In fact, one of the best learning experiences is to lose money and make mistakes.

Where Michael and his family went wrong is not correcting course after making a string of bad financial decisions. They did not start saving early. They assumed that Michael's large income would continue indefinitely thus they didn't need to worry about the future. Minimal saving led to inadequate investing. They missed out on the magic of compounding their returns. As they aged and their children grew up, they tapped their retirement funds for risky business ventures. They employed several of their children in these ventures, thus depriving their children of responsibility for their own financial futures.

They broke the cardinal money rule of taking care of one's own retirement first and foremost. Children have long earning lives; whereas middle aged adults have less time to earn and grow their own wealth.

Michael and his wife invested more in risky entrepreneurial ventures than they could afford to lose. They borrowed more than they could afford to pay back when tough economic times hit. Lifetime wealth planning requires conscious attention to balancing living for now and for later.

> **Embrace your mistakes. Everyone makes money mistakes. The rich learn from them and move on.**

This sad story highlights how intelligence and high income do not automatically lead to smart financial decision-making. Just as there are middle class earners who amass great wealth, there are high income earners who retire with little.

High intelligence and income are not required for financial security. It is the smart lifestyle and money habits that lead to wealth.

Thomas J. Stanley, PhD[2], details countless ordinary folks who've amassed extraordinary wealth in his series of books about millionaires. You can join their ranks with financially smart living.

Choose to live like the wealthy and divert part of every dollar earned to saving and investing.

THE TAKEAWAYS

Make a decision to eliminate all of your debt now. This action, although initially difficult, is crucial for long term wealth. When you continue to pay high interest payments, you cheat yourself out of tens of thousands of dollars. The credit dependent are controlled by others. The borrower can never be totally financially free. Don't let money control or enslave you.

Make smart money decisions daily. Small smart money choices lead to wealth. Remember the earlier examples where saving five dollars per day and investing that cash can turn into thousands of dollars over time? The more you practice smart money decisions, the easier it becomes.

Samir, an old friend, confided in me that he was brought up in a very economically conservative home. When he and his family went shopping as a boy, they focused on getting the most value for their money. Before dropping a dime, his parents taught him to consider whether he needed the new purchase or if something he already owned would fulfill his desire. Samir keeps his clothes in good condition, and likes to be in style. At the end of the season sales he adds to his wardrobe with one or two fashion items. By mixing the new fashions with his existing wardrobe he looks great, on a budget.

Now, Samir is an adult with a high paying sales job. Even though he can afford to regularly splurge, his earlier habits enable him to continue to spend conservatively. These ingrained financial decisions lead to economic freedom and flexibility. Instead of recklessly spending his earnings, he continues to live economically while saving and investing for the future. Samir's lifestyle habits afford him the freedom to travel, buy a home, build a family, or even retire early should he desire.

For those without economical life style habits, it takes time and practice to develop them. The multitude of folks in their fifty's, sixty's and older struggling with inadequate financial resources are a reminder of the importance of learning to live money smart.

> Set a few small goals.
> If the goals are too grand, you may become overwhelmed and fail to begin.

Set small money goals immediately. Don't let the stress of debt or the fear of money matters keep you from facing your finances. Take a baby step today. Skip the trip to the snack counter at work and grab a banana and granola bar from the kitchen cabinet.

Don't buy those lottery tickets this month, take the fifty dollars and deposit them into your investment account instead.

A 45 year old man wrote to an advice columnist and asked if he should pursue his lifelong dream of becoming a doctor, or if he was too old. The columnist replied, in four years you can be 49 years old and in the same job as you currently hold, or at age 49 you can be a doctor. Either way, you will be 49 years old. In other words, time will pass, you can choose to maximize that time and work on your most important priorities or not, but either way, you will advance in age.

I wanted to get my MBA in my twenties but pursued other opportunities instead. In midlife, I completed my MBA in finance. Did I make a mistake in waiting? It would only be a mistake if I never pursued my goal. The same can be said of saving and investing, if you have not started yet, start now. Forget about time past.

> You have the power to control the now.

Transfer part of your earnings into an investing account immediately. The longer you wait the less wealth you accumulate. Life is filled with fears and stressors, but procrastination only makes them worse. Start investing now, as time in the market is the greatest builder of long term wealth.

FOR A GREAT LIFE, DEAL HEAD-ON WITH MONEY ISSUES

In the end, life is about experiences and people, not things. Dr. Martin Seligman[3] of the Positive Psychology Center, and many others found that after your basic needs are met, more money does not equal greater happiness. Reward your success with non-financial gifts and treats. Bask in the joy of friends and family, not spending. Drown your sorrows in exercise and support from others, not shopping.

And remember, buying a lottery ticket is not investing in your future. Buying a lottery ticket is leaving your future to chance. Build strong financial habits now, and reap the rewards your entire life.

Appendix:
Great Bonus Stuff

GENERAL MONEY MANAGEMENT & CALCULATORS

Barbara Friedberg Personal Finance-Save, Invest, and Build Wealth http://barbarafriedbergpersonalfinance.com/

How to Invest and Outperform Most Active Mutual Fund Managers, Barbara Friedberg - free micro book ($9.99 value) http://forms.aweber.com/form/87/2066025387.htm

National Endowment for Financial Education http://www.nefe.org/

Help With My Bank.gov- Answers to bank, loan, credit, and more questions http://www2.helpwithmybank.gov/

Money Management; Mint.com https://www.mint.com/

Money Management; Planwise.com http://planwise.com/

Farnoosh Torabi, *Psych Yourself Rich,* (FT Press, 2010) http://amzn.to/1xjcPpI

Dr. Charles Richards, *The Psychology of Wealth,* (McGraw-Hill, 2012) http://amzn.to/1kQSLRG

Calculators; Bankrate.com http://www.bankrate.com/calculators.aspx

Calculators; FinancialMentor.com http://financialmentor.com/calculator

Jemstep Online Portfolio Management Software http://barbarafriedbergpersonalfinance.com/jemstep-review-portfolio-management-software/

Personal Capital Investment Management Software
http://barbarafriedbergpersonalfinance.com/personal-capital-review-online-investment-man

DEBT RESOURCES

Federal Trade Commission - Debt Collection FAQ
http://www.consumer.ftc.gov/articles/0149-debt-collection

Federal Trade Commission – Facts for Consumers (debt help) http://www.consumer.ftc.gov/articles/0150-coping-debt

Federal Direct Consolidation Information - Student loan consolidation http://www.loanconsolidation.ed.gov/

U. S. Department of Education student loan information - National student loan data system
https://www.nslds.ed.gov/nslds_SA/

Debt Blog and debt reduction app - The Debt Myth Blog http://www.thedebtmyth.com/

Ready for Zero- Debt Blog https://www.readyforzero.com/

SAVING RESOURCES

Online saving resource; Smarty Pig
https://www.smartypig.com/

TreasuryDirect; I Savings Bonds - Government I (inflation) Savings Bonds http://www.treasurydirect.gov/indiv/products/prod_ibonds_glance.htm

Money Saving Blog - Wise Bread
http://www.wisebread.com/resources

Automatic saving app - Saved Plus http://savedplus.com/

INVESTING RESOURCES

Barbara A. Friedberg, *How to Invest and Outperform Most Active Mutual Fund Managers* (2014)
http://forms.aweber.com/form/87/2066025387.htm

Comprehensive investment information - Investopedia
http://www.investopedia.com/

Financial education including finance, accounting, and personal finance - Money Chimp
http://www.moneychimp.com/

Charles D. Ellis and Burton G. Malkiel, *The Elements of Investing* (Wiley, 2010) http://amzn.to/TnLxyX

Zvi Bodie and Rachelle Taqqu, *Risk Less and Prosper*, (Wiley, 2012) http://amzn.to/UhVdvF

DISCOUNT BROKERS

Charles Schwab https://www.schwab

Fidelity https://www.fidelity.com/

TD Ameritrade https://www.tdameritrade.com/home.page

Vanguard; https://investor.vanguard.com/home/

NOTES

INTRODUCTION: GET STARTED NOW

1. J Cafferty. (2012, July 25). How much money would it take for you to "feel" wealthy? (Web log post). Retrieved from http://caffertyfile.blogs.cnn.com/2012/07/25/how-much-money-would-it-take-for-you-to-feel-wealthy/

2. Kahneman, D. & Deaton, A. (2010). High income improves evaluation of life but not emotional well-being (Abstract). Proceedings of the National Academy of Sciences of the United States of America, 107 (38), 16489-16493).

STEP 1: KEEP THE DEBT DEVIL FROM SWEATING YOU

1. Assumes an interest rate of 5 percent.

2. Use a credit card calculator to figure out what it will take to pay off your credit card; (www.bankrate.com/calculators/auto/auto-loan-calculator)

3. Assume returns are a bit lower than the historical averages; 9 percent for a diversified stock index mutual fund and 5 percent for a diversified bond fund. Assume you invest 60% of the funds in the stock fund and 40 percent in the bond fund.

STEP 2: SAVING-THE PATH TO MORE BENJAMIN'S

1. Venti, S.F. & Wise, D. A. Chioce, chance, and wealth dispersion at retirement (NBER working paper no. 27521) Retrieved from SSRN: http://ssrn.com/abstract=216449

2. Government I Bonds can be purchased online at http:// www.treasurydirect.gov/indiv/research/ indepth/ ibonds/res_ibonds.htm. Each individual can purchase up to $10,000 worth of these bonds annually.

3. Sign up to receive a free micro book *How to Invest and Outperform Most Active Mutual Fund Managers*, http://forms.aweber.com/form/ 87/2066025387.htm for a research supported investment approach. Subscription includes free Wealth Tips Newsletter.

4. Norris, M. (2012, June). "Not everyone can read proof: The legacy of Lu Burke. The New Yorker. Retrieved from http://www.newyorker.com/ online/blogs/books/2012/06/ lu-burke-new-yorker-southbury-library.html

STEP 3: SPEND YOUR WAY TO AN AWESOME LIFE

1. Linfield, L.E. (2011). 2010 Annual consumer bankruptcy demographics report: A five year perspective of the American debtor. *Social Science Research Network, Institute for financial Literacy*. Abstract retrieved from http://ssrn.com/abstract=1925006.

STEP 4: GET A COOL CRIB CHEAP

1. Friedberg, B.A. (2012, January 27). A strategy to save a bundle; The train conductor's money saving tip (Web log post). Retrieved from http://barbarafriedbergpersonalfinance.com/strategy-save-money-saving-tip-from-train-conductor/.

2. Cuban, M (2011, August 5). Mark Cuban on how to get rich. *Business Insider.* Retrieved from http://articles.businessinsider.com/2011-08-05/strategy/29958437_1_ get-rich-markets-credit.

STEP 5: STUFF HAPPENS-PROTECT YOURSELF FROM LOSS

1. Kapoor, J., Dlabay, L., Hughes, R.J. (2008) *Personal finance, 9th edition.* McGraw-Hill/Irwin.

STEP 6: BE A PORTFOLIO PLAYER! I HAVE NO MONEY INVESTING STRATEGY

1. This example assumes the portfolio earns 7 percent average annual return. The 7 percent annualized portfolio return is projected from historical returns for combined stock and bond index funds. Your returns may be different, based on future investment returns.

2. This website provides all the information you need to understand and invest in Government I Bonds and Treasury Inflation protected securities, http://www. treasurydirect.gov/.

3. Sign up to receive a free micro book *How to Invest and Outperform Most Active Mutual Fund Managers,*

http://forms.aweber.com/form/87/2066025387.htm
for a research supported investment approach.
Subscription includes free Wealth Tips Newsletter.

STEP 7: SECRETS OF THE RICH

1. National Center for education Statistics Website.
   Digest of education statistics. 2011 tables and figures.
   Retrieved from http://nces.ed.gov/ programs/
   digest/d11/tables/ dt11_397.asp

2. Indivigio, D. (2011, May 11). Chart of the day: 9%
   of Americans are millionaires in 2011. *The Atlantic.*
   Retrieved from http://www.theatlantic.com
   /business/ archive/2011/05/chart-of-the-day-9-of-
   americans-are- millionaires-in-2011/238458/

3. Employment projections; *Education pays.* (2011).
   Bureau of Labor Statistics Website. Retrieved from
   http://www.bls.gov/emp/ep_chart_001.htm

4. Davis-Laack, P. (2012, October 16). 10 Things
   happy people do differently. *Psychology Today.*
   Retrieved from
   http://www.psychologytoday.com/blog/pressure-
   proof/201210/10-things-happy-people-do-
   differently

5. Spector, D., Lubin, G. and Kelley, M.B. (2012, April
   6). 18 Signs That the Lottery Is Preying On
   Americas Poor. *Business Insider.* Retrieved from
   http://www.businessinsider.com/lottery-is-a-tax-
   on-the-poor-2012-4?op=1

STEP 8: SHORT AND SWEET SUMMARY

1. Winter, D. (2006, February 24). Financial planners: Winning the lottery isn't always a dream. *Lincoln Journal Star.* Retrieved from http://journalstar.com/special-section/news/financial-planners-winning-the- lottery-isn-t-always-a-dream/article_ecba141b-3e59- 5914-a321-38b4adb20733.html

2. The website of Thomas J. Stanley, PhD includes countless resources regarding the wealthy, http://www. thomasjstanley.com/.

3. The University of Pennsylvania website of Dr. Martin Seligman's Authentic Happiness project explores the field of positive psychology and studies the causes of happiness http://www.authentichappiness.sas.upenn.

Barbara Friedberg Personal Finance
http://barbarafriedbergpersonalfinance.com
Save, Invest, and Build Wealth

I welcome your comments –
Contact Barbara Friedberg at;
http://barbarafriedbergpersonalfinance.com/contact/

Free Bonus: *How to Invest and Outperform Most Active Mutual Fund Managers* ($9.99 value).
(http://forms.aweber.com/form/87/2066025387.htm)

This book is dedicated to Bob, Rebecca, Helen and Harry.

ISBN: 978-0-9888555-1-9

60837406R00069

Made in the USA
Lexington, KY
20 February 2017